60

FARRAR
STRAUS
GIROUX

THE HISTORY BOYS: THE FILM

THE HISTORY BOYS

THE FILM

Alan Bennett
and
Nicholas Hytner

Adapted from the original stage play by Alan Bennett

Faber and Faber, Inc.

An affiliate of Farrar, Straus and Giroux

New York

Faber and Faber, Inc.
An affiliate of Farrar, Straus and Giroux
19 Union Square West, New York 10003

Printed in the United States of America
Originally published in 2006 by Faber and Faber Limited, Great Britain
Published in the United States by Faber and Faber, Inc.
First American edition, 2006

Grateful acknowledgement is made for permission to reprint the following material:
'Loveliest of trees, the cherry now' and 'On Wenlock Edge the wood's in trouble',
by A. E. Housman, by permission of the Society of Authors as the Literary
Representative of the Estate of A. E. Housman; 'MCMXIV', by Philip Larkin,
copyright © 1964 by the Estate of Philip Larkin, by permission of Faber and Faber
Limited; 'Musée des Beaux Arts' and 'Lullaby', copyright 1940 and renewed © 1968 by
W. H. Auden, from *Collected Poems* by W. H. Auden, used by permission of Random
House, Inc.; 'Voices against England in the Night', by Stevie Smith, by permission
of the Estate of James MacGibbon. The extract from *Brief Encounter* is
used by courtesy of Carlton International.

Library of Congress Control Number: 2006933956
ISBN-13: 978-0-86547-971-5
ISBN-10: 0-86547-971-2

www.fsgbooks.com

3   5   7   9   10   8   6   4   2

CONTENTS

The History Boys is the second film that Alan Bennett and I have made together. The first, in 1994, was *The Madness of King George*. Both started as plays at the National Theatre, though *The Madness of King George* had its title helpfully changed on the journey from stage to screen, as it was feared that for an audience unversed in the history of the English monarchy the title of the play – *The Madness of George III* – might imply it was the sequel to *The Madness of George 1* and *The Madness of George 2*.

Despite the shortcomings of its title, there always seemed to be a film in *The Madness of George III*. It was shaped like a screenplay, and stage directions like 'Outside St Paul's Cathedral' and 'Inside the Royal Apartments, Windsor' required more than a customary suspension of disbelief from the theatre audience. The film was able to provide King George with a court to preside over and a country to rule. Shooting it, we travelled all over England, and watching Nigel Hawthorne gallop his horse towards the camera in Windsor Great Park, it was impossible not to believe that the story had found its intended medium.

It took us longer to believe that *The History Boys* belonged on screen. It probably wasn't until we first put it in front of nine hundred people that we fully realised there was an audience for it in the theatre. I'd been nagging Alan Bennett for a play since my appointment as the National's director in 2001. It arrived, as his plays always do, out of the blue, in the autumn of 2003; and although I was dazzled by its wit and erudition, and by the urgency of its discussion of the purpose of education and the nature of historical truth, I reckoned there were maybe only seventy or eighty performances in it. I think I worried that it might turn out to be too esoteric for a larger public.

The first preview crowd at the National, however, comprehensively trashed the old adage that nobody ever made a fortune by overestimating the intelligence of the audience. Like all subsequent audiences, they went happily nuts. Exhilarated by the play's subject matter and often convulsed with laughter at its jokes, they rose to it above all because they cared about its people; which suggested there might be a film in it after all.

We knew our show's strengths, and though they included neither a driving narrative nor any whiff of the picturesque, there seemed to be no point in trying to parachute into the material cinematic attributes it had no interest in possessing. If there was ever to be a *History Boys* film, the point of it would surely be that it would allow us to intensify what was exciting about the play. Maybe it could bring us closer to the protagonists, get under their skins and see behind their eyes. Maybe it could capture their speed of thought and the glitter of their intellects. But whatever else it turned out to be, it would be about eight boys and four teachers. So when we finally started to think about making it, we knew it would also be about the twelve actors who had created them.

The casting question surfaced as soon as we began talking with potential financiers. Film companies understandably want to cover themselves for the near inevitable failure of a film to meet expectations. They reason that the best way of persuading audiences to see a film is to stuff it with actors they want to see, whatever the film turns out to be. It would be nice to think that what audiences want to see is a good film, whoever's in it. This utopian way of looking at things, though widely shared by those who make films, is treated with grave suspicion by those who finance them. The first film company we spoke to wanted to make what might be called a contribution to the casting process. As we already had a cast that we thought unimprovable, and whose ownership of their roles after a year on stage was absolute, this got us nowhere.

I am fiercely proud of the eight history boys. Three of them – Samuel Barnett, Dominic Cooper and Russell Tovey – had been at the National for some time, their versatility matched now by an authority that had grown with each passing week. While appearing in our vast adaptation of Philip Pullman's *His Dark Materials*, they had all taken part in the first exploratory reading of *The History Boys*. Jamie Parker was also part of the group that read the play for the first time, playing Rudge. He did Rudge well, but later did Scripps even better, and turned out to be a genuinely accomplished pianist, which was a massive bonus. It was late in the day that we realised Russell Tovey should play Rudge. Russell had come to the National to play the Boy in *Henry V*, and had since established a monopoly in fresh-faced enthusiasts, which is what he is in life. Rudge couldn't be further away from the real Russell, who readily rose to the challenge of showing us how restricted our idea of him had been. Samuel Anderson, James Corden, Sacha Dhawan and

Andrew Knott joined us at the start of rehearsals in March 2004 and, by the time we opened, all eight played together like a jazz band. I have never known actors so in sympathy with each other, so quick to generate between each other real thought and feeling, and to erase the distinction between theatrical illusion and life.

This was no small achievement. Alan Bennett is a stylist as recognisable, in his way, as Oscar Wilde. People don't actually talk the way they do in his plays: the history boys are often far wittier and more articulate than even the cleverest Oxbridge entrant. It was a measure not only of their exceptional talent but also of the work we did together over several weeks of rehearsal and many months of performance that the eight actors were able to root Alan's inimitable speech patterns in concrete reality and toss them off without apparent effort. 'Lecher though one is, or aspires to be,' says Dakin, aged eighteen, referring to Hector's extra-curricular activities, 'it occurs to me that the lot of woman cannot be easy, who must suffer such inexpert male fumblings virtually on a daily basis.' Dominic Cooper delivers this with the aplomb of a latter-day Jack Worthing, but you never doubt that it's part of the daily banter of a Sheffield teenager, falling as naturally from his lips as the cheerful obscenities that pepper all the boys' dialogue on screen, as it would in life.

As for the teachers: Richard Griffiths, Frances de la Tour and Clive Merrison were National Theatre veterans, and it had been obvious from the moment the play arrived that we should be pursuing them to be in it. Irwin was the trickiest part to cast, his oscillations between intellectual self-confidence and personal insecurity baffling to most of the actors who read for it. Stephen Campbell Moore arrived in the nick of time, only a couple of weeks before rehearsals started.

My attachment and Alan's to these actors went beyond personal loyalty. The world we had created together was the world we wanted to film. There was undoubtedly another, and maybe a better, film that could have been made based on Alan's play, but none of us had any interest in it. So we decided to cut loose and make by ourselves all the decisions that would under normal circumstances involve consultation with our paymasters. We'd go looking for someone to pay for the movie only when we were ready to start shooting it.

We realised immediately that we'd only get away with this if we were able to offer the film at the kind of price that would be relatively untroubling to those who might sign the cheque. Knowing next to nothing about film finance, I plucked out of the ether a figure of £1.5 million and asked Kevin Loader and Damian Jones to join us to produce a budget. Expert in the making of low-budget movies, they quickly set a ceiling of £2 million and worked out how not to exceed it.

Inevitably, the first economy was in the size of everybody's pay packet. We would have to ask the cast and every member of the team we were now gathering around us to work for much less than their market rate, and to invite them in return to be partners in the ownership of the film, so that if it was a success they could all share in it. It was no surprise that the actors, committed as they were to what we'd all made together, enthusiastically signed up; though they might have been less sanguine if they'd known that our parsimony would ultimately extend to their dressing arrangements on the set, and that they'd be changing for the day's shoot in whatever classroom happened to be available, occasionally sharing it with the schoolboy extras who would otherwise have been using it for a geography lesson. That the rest of the crew were ready to work with us for so little was a tribute to their generosity of spirit, and to their recognition that when an Alan Bennett screenplay comes along, it's worth crossing the road for.

Delivering the screenplay seemed less of a problem to me than it did to Alan. I'd been full of ideas about turning *George III* into a screenplay, most of them designed to demonstrate that I was a *bona fide* film director, my imagination no longer confined by the proscenium arch. If there was half a chance to move the camera, or to cut to a different location, I took it. The best scenes were nevertheless lifted more or less verbatim from the play.

This time, I started out by offering Alan very little beyond a conviction that we shouldn't try to open out something that worked precisely because it was enclosed. Closed worlds can be as eloquent on film as they are on stage. Schools, prisons, hospitals, courtrooms: they all operate according to easily graspable rules and stand as microcosms of the wider world. Alan worried that he didn't have much to add to the play; I was glad that he didn't. My models were the great Hollywood play adaptations of the mid-twentieth century. *The Front Page*, *The Philadelphia Story* and *A Streetcar Named Desire* waste no effort on straying from the centre. Their energy springs from the dynamic exploration of small worlds that are fully inhabited by large spirits.

In the event, Alan's first draft included some marvellously inventive new material. Some we kept because it brought us closer to the people at the centre, some simply because it was so entertaining. The gym teacher and the art teacher are strictly speaking extraneous, but we all liked them too much to care. Much of the new stuff, however, didn't make it to the second draft because it didn't seem necessary. The finished screenplay re-imagined some of the material of the play for the camera, but left large swathes of it untouched. The challenge was to find a way of shooting it that responded to the crackling intellectual energy of the history lessons; to Hector's determined subjection of the boys to the popular culture of his own youth; to the surging sexual undercurrents of Dakin's and Irwin's mutual obsession; to the still centre of the film when Hector and Posner unwittingly open themselves over a reading of 'Drummer Hodge'. I reckoned if we could devote seven minutes of film to the teaching of a poem by Thomas Hardy we'd be doing OK. Watching now as Sam Barnett and Richard Griffiths slowly recognise 'a sense of not sharing, of being out of it – a holding back. Not being in the swim,' I know why we made the movie. Freed from the necessity of including nine hundred people nightly into their conversation, these two marvellous actors played only for each other and allowed the camera the most intimate imaginable access to a profoundly felt loneliness.

My key partner was the director of photography, Andrew Dunn. Andrew had shot *The Madness of King George*, and had transformed me from a helpless novice into someone who at least thought he knew what he was doing. I was asking him now to collaborate on an entirely different enterprise. To meet the budget, we needed to shoot *The History Boys* in six weeks – a lightning quick schedule for a film, but one that I thought we could make because the actors could not have been more in command of their material. Even if we'd had the resources, I didn't want to make the kind of film we'd made in 1994. *King George* involved the animation of a world familiar from the paintings of Zoffany and Reynolds; it was about people whose lives and identities were bound up in lavish displays of power and wealth. The world of *The History Boys* – a modest Yorkshire grammar school in the 1980s – was remote from the court of George III not just for the obvious reasons. The spirit of the boys who populate it is immediate and spontaneous, and though they often think and speak with theatrical elegance, the concrete reality of their lives is rough and ready.

Andrew responded with the same invention that he'd brought to the regal splendour of George III's Windsor, but where he had then conjured up a folk memory of monarchy, he now photographed a real memory of school. I've seen films set in schools that look the way films look; *The History Boys* looks the way schools look. It was useful that this was cheaper than the glossier alternative; it also seemed right.

We had a script, a cast, a budget, a schedule and a team standing by to start by the time my fellow producers and our agent Anthony Jones went to Cannes to find the money. Every aspect of the film was a *fait accompli* apart from who was going to pay for it, and we fully expected our intransigence about what we wanted to make to be a major stumbling block. In the event, it was a sellers' market, the lure of an Alan Bennett screenplay yet again proving to be irresistible. A partnership of Byzantine complexity between the BBC, DNA Films and Fox Searchlight was thrashed out on the Croisette, and explained to me when the team returned to London. I still don't understand it.

Armed at last with a chequebook, we were able to look for a school. The film is set in the eighties, at a time when Hector's style of teaching was still (just) imaginable, before the dictates of the curriculum and the target culture had all but buried it. The design brief was specific: we needed a pre-war grammar school with sixties or seventies additions. I had my own school, Manchester Grammar, in mind; Alan had his – Leeds Modern. Both of us had been through exactly what the history boys go through: the extra term, after A-Levels, spent in preparation for the entrance exams to Oxford and Cambridge (something else that disappeared in the eighties). After the elaborate research that had gone into *The Madness of King George*, it seemed almost embarrassingly straightforward, and Watford Boys' Grammar School fitted the bill in nearly every respect, particularly after it had been deftly remodelled by John Beard. We stayed there, and at Watford Girls' Grammar School (which offered more evocative interiors than the boys' school), for five of our six weeks. We spent the sixth week in Yorkshire, shooting just enough, we hoped, to locate our fictional school somewhere near Sheffield, though the views of Sheffield in the film are in fact of Halifax, which looks more like Sheffield ought to look than Sheffield does. The shoot ended aptly enough in Oxford, where the history boys were able to see what all the fuss had been about. They were sceptical, which would have pleased Hector.

Every day of the shoot was marked by the authority of a group of actors who had been playing together for a year, and by their evident satisfaction that they could now play for each other and allow the camera to come to them. I hope the result is a film that, even when it follows the same script as the play, often seems to be saying something more. On stage, the central argument can seem unfairly weighted in Hector's favour, as if there were no disputing Housman's dictum, quoted in Hector's first lesson, that 'all knowledge is precious whether or not it serves the slightest human use'. The truth is that much of what Hector teaches is entirely self-indulgent; and his insistence on inflicting on his class the culture, high and low, of his own youth is at least questionable. In performance, however, all Hector's stuff, particularly when it's done with the kind of élan that James Corden and Andrew Knott bring to their rendition of the end of *Now, Voyager*, is irresistible. In the film, Stephen Campbell Moore's Irwin provides Hector with truly formidable opposition, seductive enough to allay the suspicion that there's a thin line between a sparkling intellect and a flashy one. More than that, Stephen peels off an extra layer of skin for the camera and reveals an unexpected vulnerability that belies his intellectual arrogance.

It was a repeated pleasure to watch rushes and see in detailed close-up how completely individual each of the history boys was, even in scenes where they operate in a pack. Samuel Anderson's quiet irony and Sacha Dhawan's quick wit seem as vivid to me as the frustrated ambition of Clive Merrison's constantly wrong-footed Headmaster, who has much more to say than them (and who says it with consummate panache). The mystery of Frances de la Tour's performance, however, survived even the tightest close-up. It seems entirely effortless; but the effortlessness of the best actors is always the result of an art that conceals art.

There is a scene that didn't make it beyond the first draft of the screenplay, and was even cut eventually from the play, though only in the interests of brevity and with a heavy heart, because like so much of Alan's discarded material, it was better than most writers' highlights. In it, Rudge challenged Hector to recognise a song by the Pet Shop Boys; Hector, ignorant of all popular culture after about 1950, was completely floored. 'You can't expect him to know that,' said Timms. 'And anyway, it's crap.' 'So is Gracie Fields,' said Rudge, 'only that's his crap. This is our crap.' I feel something similar about *The History Boys*. I have no idea yet whether it's a good film, but it's our film.

NICHOLAS HYTNER
National Theatre, February 2006

14 July 2005   Nick H. picks me up at 8.45 and by a roundabout route the bombed bus in Tavistock Place has made necessary, we go painfully through the traffic-choked streets down to the National and the first reading of the film script of *The History Boys*.

As always I'm startled by the size of the crew and the number of people in attendance, the beginning of a film like the conferences planning the Normandy landings. It's lovely to see all the cast again, though, and to hear the script read, what new jokes there are going down well. I read in for Frances de la T. who's away on holiday and there's some talk of my playing a don in one of the Oxford scenes. But not if I can help it.

17 July   Yesterday to Broughton Castle where we filmed part of *The Madness of King George*. We have our sandwiches on the edge of a field of flax scattered with poppies, the earth of the cart track so rich and red the scene seems almost absurdly rural. So, too, does Broughton itself and, though there are quite a few visitors, it's not besieged as it was when I first saw it ten years ago by all the trunks and tents and paraphernalia of a film crew.

The lady of the house, Marietta Say, is helping to show people around. She's cheerful and downright as ever, and when I tell her I'm about to start another film with Nicholas Hytner she says that though he's very clever as a director she secretly prefers directors who are less accomplished as they are more likely to overrun, in which case the estate will get more money.

There are good unseen bits in this lovely house, like a plain room at the top of a staircase tower where the campaign against Charles I is said to have been plotted and which gives onto the leads, where one can walk, a privilege not accorded in any other country house that I've come across.

I am writing this up at a desk in a room at Watford Boys' Grammar School, which is dressed as Mrs Lintott's classroom for the filming of *The History Boys*, which started this morning.

I feel a bit lost, as so often when filming, where the author has no ordained place or prescribed function, and with nothing useful to do except gossip and make myself amiable, I succumb all too readily to the lure of conviviality and sociability's powerful drug and just sit around and watch. Our boys, with make-up, look satisfyingly younger than their real Watford Grammar School counterparts who are themselves part of 'directed action' and on cue play loudly (and quite violently) on the field outside.

I come away at three o'clock, my only contribution today to give Stephen Campbell Moore the correct pronunciation of 'prepuce'.

21 July A touch of writer's paranoia this morning. The trickiest and in some ways the most shocking scene in the play is the sixth-former Dakin's virtual seduction of Irwin, the young supply teacher. It's a difficult scene to play because Irwin, warned by the older schoolmaster, Hector, not to make a fool of himself over the boy, resists Dakin's (very specific) advances throughout the scene until he suddenly caves in and they fix up a date.

Why does he cave in? Partly because Dakin is, literally, irresistible: apart from being good-looking, his will is much stronger than Irwin's and where sex is concerned he has all the know-how. On stage, though it was always a gripping scene, it wasn't always plain what prompted Irwin's surrender, and so in the film script I have given this a physical trigger and at the point where Irwin is wavering I make Dakin touch him.

Chatting to Stephen Campbell Moore (Irwin) and Dominic Cooper (Dakin) yesterday, I discover that having rehearsed the scene they are to do no touching. Normally Nick H. would tell me of any departure from the script and since it's seldom we disagree there's no problem. This time, though, he hasn't and I wonder if it's because he knows I feel quite strongly about it. At any rate it will have to be talked through before the scene is shot.

Waiting for my car to pick me up this morning I rehearse what I need to say about the scene, the only one in the play in which anyone comes even close to getting their heart's desire, so that Dakin's hand on Irwin's chest or his belly, as I've actually written it, is highly charged. The car is late and I know the scene will have been set up by now and perhaps even be shooting. I telephone to find no car has been ordered and one won't be free for half an hour. I sit there waiting, wondering if this is deliberate and a way of forestalling any objections I might have and avoiding the inevitable confrontation.

When I eventually get to the set they have indeed rehearsed the scene and done at least one take (with no touching). I say that some sort of physical contact seems to me essential, but the actors can't make it work though I still think that what I've suggested, Dakin's finger idly sliding inside Irwin's shirt, would do it. What also works, though, is a much longer pause before Irwin surrenders and this, finally, is what we settle for . . . though whether the pause will survive in the editing I'm not sure.

Of course there has been no plot to keep me off the set while the scene is shot and I laugh about it afterwards. But I can think of other playwrights who would need more reassurance on that point than I do, and who would make more of a fuss about any divergence from what they've written.

The other lurking fear I have about scenes like this – and which ties in with Posner's view in the play – is that where sex is concerned, directors think I'm not that sort of writer (just as Posner is thought not that sort of boy), and so don't entirely trust what I've written. It's one of the reasons I took to writing the occasional short story because in that form I could express myself without let or hindrance.

(It's interesting, though, that when I later watch the dress rehearsal of the second cast doing the stage version I have exactly the same feeling about the scene, namely that it needs some sort of touch. Maybe that's what the audience is feeling also and it not happening is one reason why the scene works.)

Because of the shot Sam Anderson has to move his desk. 'Don't tell me. It's black boys to the back again.'

We eat our lunch on picnic tables outside the classroom in a huge tearing wind that topples the glasses and snatches away the plates. The school proper broke up at noon and the vast playing field is deserted, the high suburban trees roaring in the wind. I wander across the empty grass feeling as once I did fifty and more years ago when I was in my own last days at school. Meanwhile our boys play football against the playground wall with an openness and abandon I have never managed in all my life.

23 July Though I knew there would not be time in the film to see the home lives of the boys, I was hoping we would be able to include a brief collage of their various parents.

Lockwood, I thought, would come from a poor background; his mother is a single parent, and while wanting him to go on to university doesn't know how it is to be paid for. Thus he is seen at the start of the film working in the holidays as a milkman; he goes up for the scholarship interview in his trainers and ends up enlisting in the army as this will pay for him to go to Oxford.

Whereas we never see Mrs Lockwood, we do get glimpses of some of the other parents, a few of whom were going to have a line or two. Mrs Scripps for instance, who is uncomfortable with her son's piety. ('I said to him, "Jesus is such a bad role model. You'd be better off with somebody like Paul McCartney."') Mrs Dakin: 'He's full of this new master. Sexual intercourse seems to have taken a back seat.' And Mrs Crowther: 'He's a lovely-looking lad. Get him in a bathing costume and he'd walk it. And these posh places, black isn't necessarily a handicap. It can be a plus.'

MR TIMMS (*waking up*) I went through Oxford once. Shocking traffic.

Significantly the only parents wholeheartedly in favour of their son going on to Oxford or Cambridge are the Asian Mr and Mrs Akhtar, though even there not without reservations.

MR AKHTAR I gather it is the centre court of English ideas.
MRS AKHTAR But we do not want a Mr Smart Arse.
MR AKHTAR Oh no, my love.
MRS AKHTAR We've got one of those already.

These scenes survived until the penultimate rewrite, when they had to be cut on grounds of length. We get occasional glimpses (the Akhtars turning up in force for the posting of the A-level results), but the film like the play is about school and the outside world scarcely figures.

24 July Seeing Hector off on the bike for what turns out to be his last ride, the boys are not in school uniform but in their own clothes. It's no fault of the designer but it's curious how this blurs their characters. In school uniform, white shirts and ties, blazers and dark trousers, each character is clearly defined. Put into civvies they lose their edge and some of their attraction. James Corden in sweater and trousers looks, so he says, like White Van Man. Dominic, in white T-shirt and black leather jacket, looks straight out of a sixties Cliff Richard movie and Posner, in sports coat and corduroys, seems to have been dressed like me . . . which I don't mind, though I'm not sure it suits him or his character.

What is certain is that all of them look better and more interesting in uniform than in their own clothes.

I've come across this once or twice before – with orchestras, for instance (better in evening dress) and with waiters. The staff of The Odeon in New York were dashing and aloof in their restaurant rig, but catch them going home at two in the morning and they had shrunk to the drab, the camp and the ordinary creatures the uniform disguised.

28 July Watch the first love scene between Dakin and Fiona, the Headmaster's secretary, shot in a suburban house just up the road from school. It is not especially intimate, with no nudity at this stage, though I'd expected Dakin's trousers to be open as, since they're lying on the bed and it's quite heavy snogging, they presumably would be. However I don't suggest it as it seems prurient.

Later we film the second scene when Dakin, fully clothed, is talking about Irwin while Fiona waits for him to come to bed. This configuration came to me at a Sickert exhibition in the Abbot Hall Gallery in Kendal, where there was a painting from the Camden Town murder series in which a clothed and threatening man, possibly a client, stands by the bed of a woman whom he is about to fuck or kill, or both.

Though hardly so dramatic, our scene takes a long time to film, but only because the sound of Dakin's falling trousers keeps obscuring the lines. I suggest to John Midgley on sound that Dominic be asked to hold the line until he's got his trousers off but John, who has obviously had some unfortunate experiences with actors, thinks this will only cause more problems. So we go to thirteen takes until the trousers just happen to come down before the line is said, the gate is checked and we go on to a scene on the football pitch. All rather wasted because the scene is eventually cut and with it the two lines which I like as, in half-a-dozen words, they wholly explain Dakin's relation to Irwin.

DAKIN I want him to rate me.
FIONA Rape you?
DAKIN Rate. *Rate.*

1 August A change of location. We film the first of Hector's classroom scenes at Watford Girls' Grammar School, an older establishment than the boys' equivalent and one more appropriate to the piece. There are parquet floors not unlike the corridors of my own school, Leeds Modern, fifty years ago; the walls are lined with team photographs dating back to the twenties, and it's such a pleasingly old-fashioned place I imagine our set-dressers must have been at work. In fact it's all the genuine article with some of the fixtures and fittings (the brass and bakelite door handles for instance) so antique as to make it surprising they have survived.

2 August   Film the French class. Always the funniest scene in the theatre, it's hard to transfer its mischief to film. On stage one of the best moments is the arrival of Irwin and the Headmaster in the middle of Hector's class acting out a scene in a brothel, with Dakin standing there in his shirt tails. The audience sees Hector and Irwin waiting to come in, while at the same time not being sure this is what they are meant to see. It gives them a stolen foretaste of what is to come and they begin laughing before even the Headmaster has made his entrance. On film this can to some extent be achieved by cutting to the Headmaster and Irwin coming down the corridor, but what's lost is the furtive sneak-preview sense you get on stage.

The days get hotter and a species of air-conditioning is rigged up consisting of a noisy pump connected to a long coiling silver-foil covered pipe, the opening of which is so huge it looks likely to suck in the unwary.

3 August   A difficult day. We are filming a long corridor scene in which Mrs Lintott comes up the stairs and encounters Irwin, with whom she stops to chat about Hector. Boys run up the stairs, whom she absent-mindedly slows down (a hand on the shoulder, a touch on the head . . . all things teachers are not supposed to do nowadays) and they walk on together, the scene ending at the door of Hector's classroom with Mrs Lintott denouncing the Headmaster.

'Twat, twat, twat,' she says, the last 'twat' picked up by Timms (James Corden) who, taking it to refer to him, mumbles, 'Yes, miss,' and looks suitably sheepish.

With so many elements involved the shot takes most of the morning. Frances de la T. and Stephen C. M. sometimes get to the door too soon, the passing schoolboys are too animated or sometimes not animated enough. Made to troop up and down the corridor time and time again, they end up looking as grim as the creatures in Daumier's etching of a prison yard.

Another difficulty is that today Archie Powell and his camera crew are here to pick up shots for my *South Bank Show*. Someone sensible and less self-conscious than I am would manufacture an opportunity to catch me in conversation with Nick H. over some point arising out of the shot. But nothing occurs so half the time they have nothing to film, or nothing to film involving me anyway.

Later on the boys are playing football and, the cameras nowhere in sight, I wander round the field, glad to be outside. By the time, though, I've got to the border of trees, the camera has materialised from nowhere, filming the football and me lonely as a cloud-ing in the background. And that will, I fear, be how the story is told . . . solitary ageing author a spectator at the games of the young.

4 August   Today we film the heart of the play, the scene between Hector and Posner in which the boy recites Hardy's 'Drummer Hodge' and Hector talks about the poem. Richard G. and Sam B. rehearse the scene for the benefit of Andrew Dunn and the camera crew, but so quietly I can scarcely hear what they are saying. It is shorter than on the stage (all the references to Larkin, for instance, omitted) but uncut are the lines: 'The best moments in reading are when you come across something – a thought, a feeling, a way of looking at things – which you had thought special and particular to you. Now here it is, set down by someone else, a person you have never met, someone even who is long dead. And it is as if a hand has come out and taken yours.'

This speech I only put in as an afterthought as I'd had it written for nearly thirty years, first delivering it one December night in 1977 as part of the radio programme *With Great Pleasure*. It was recorded at a parish hall somewhere in the depths of Somerset on a very foggy night and the audience so small that canned applause had to be added at the editing.

9 August   What music we should use is decided initially by Nick H. reading out a list of songs for the boys to approve. The Smiths they like (whom at least I have heard of) and anything by Kate Bush; any songs that have been in *Billy Elliot* are automatically ruled out, and Madness too (whom I also like). But whereas most of the songs I have never heard of, the boys have only to hear the title before they can reel off the words with an accompanying routine as it's the music they've grown up with.

This morning *Vogue* comes to take a photograph of the cast, and they pose, unnaturally still and stern, with one shot on their own, another with Frances de la Tour and a final one with me.

I first had my photograph in *Vogue* in 1960 when Peter Cook, Jonathan Miller, Dudley Moore and I were put in a Daimler (the first I had ever been in) and taken out to Acton where we were pictured with our coat collars up against a power station in Park Royal . . . a fashionably gritty photograph that made us look more like a pop group than young men putting on a revue.

No better at having my picture taken now than I was then, and never having learned to put it on (as the boys do as a matter of course); instead I still endeavour to look like myself, whatever that is. Somehow sincere, I suppose.

As I sit outside the arts block writing this the school groundsman brings me a bowl of mulberries from a two-hundred-year-old tree in the garden.

11 August The car comes early so I'm in time to see Dom and Jamie doing the corridor scene in which Jamie tells Dom that just because he's grateful to Irwin for getting him through the examination doesn't mean he should offer Irwin unfettered access to his dick. Jamie is peaking too soon in the sequence 'Give him a subscription to the *Spectator* or a box of Black Magic,' both over-emphasised, with the dick a bit of an anti-climax. So I'm able to point this out and feel, as so seldom, that I've been of some use.

17 August A scene in the school gymnasium, the girls' gymnasium not the boys', as, like the rest of the school, it's more old-fashioned, so much so that even the equipment – 'the apparatus', as it was always called – has scarcely changed since I was a boy. It's like revisiting the chamber in which one was tortured years ago: here are the long, brightly varnished forms, the ropes, the wall-bars, the tiered box . . . always a bad moment when another tier was added . . . against the unyielding side of which I invariably thumped my crotch.

But of course it's also toys, and before and between takes the boys swing on the ropes and vault over the horse though they can't do what the script actually requires them to do, namely to hang upside down on the wall-bars. So PE Master Adrian Scarborough's line, 'Oxford and Cambridge won't want a boy that can't hang upside down on the wall-bars,' has to be cut. The boys get some teen-movie mileage out of being in a girls' shower room, the changing rooms to me as a boy as much a place of torment as the gym itself.

The gym at my school was the province of an oldish master, Mr King, not quite a thoroughgoing sadist (he played the viola in the school orchestra) but an expert at catching you on the side of the head with a well-aimed gym shoe. Early in 1952 the rumour went round that Mr King had died very suddenly. Hope turned to exultation when the whole school was summoned to an extraordinary afternoon assembly. However, hearts sank when there, large as life, at his music stand and sawing away at the National Anthem, was Mr King. Whereupon the Headmaster stood up to announce the death not of Mr King but, far less excitingly, of the King himself. I suppose we were sorry, but George VI was always a shadowy figure and not much loved, though this at least could be said for His Majesty: he wasn't wont to catch you unexpectedly on the side of the head with a well-aimed gym shoe.

15 August Hector's memorial service, with the boys singing 'Bye Bye Blackbird' against a screen showing Hector at various stages of his life. I first saw this scene on stage at the play's dress rehearsal, when the conjunction of the song and the (unexpected) photographs brought me close to tears, and whenever I saw it during the run it retained its pathos. On screen, though, this may be hard to recapture as it must depend on when the pictures of the young Hector are seen or cut to.

The memorial service is hard to shoot, not least because the school hall is filled with schoolboy extras, who chatter and are soon bored, and though Nick H. does his best to damp them down the boys' natural exuberance, inappropriate in the circumstances, keeps breaking through.

The scene is tricky, too, in that it involves talking to the camera. This is easily done on the stage but much harder to bring off on film: sometimes it works, sometimes not, though without it always being obvious why. Nick shoots an alternative version in which most of the talking to camera (and the information thus conveyed) is done as dialogue and this seems to work better.

Still it's a lengthy job and as we do more and more takes the schoolboys, not understanding why they are having to do it again, start groaning when another take is announced and applauding when it's finished. The PAs are powerless to control them and what we need, I suppose, is a figure like that of the Headmaster in the film who can scare the shit out of them.

16 August The actors are normally picked up first thing by car and taken out to Watford and then, when we have finished shooting, taken home. It's easy enough in a morning, but the journey home can be much slower and so some of them have taken to going by train, as I do, Watford to Euston only a twenty-minute ride.

Sacha Dhawan is an Asian actor from Manchester and Sam Anderson from London is of mixed race. Coming home together this last week they were both stopped and searched at Euston. Quite cool about it, they also found it funny, though Sacha says that having to spread and be searched as commuters hurried by is a bit shy-making. Nor do the police seem to know what they are looking for. Sacha writes poetry and has kept a diary of the filming, and having been told that they were actors, the police go through his diary and question them about the film, though less in the interests of counter-terrorism, Sacha felt, than as readers of *Hello* magazine.

Today I travelled to Euston with Sacha, rather hoping he would be stopped again so that I could see the process at first-hand. But for the first time in a fortnight there are no policemen at the station.

On another day (and not with Sacha, fortunately) I overhear a genial-looking middle-aged workman, a builder possibly, chatting on his mobile. 'No, we're moving, hadn't you heard? Well, we're getting outnumbered where we are, know what I mean?'

18 August En route through Wembley yesterday to the location at Harrow, we kept passing schools and colleges with the pupils standing about waiting or, in one case, just having received their A-level results. Today we film the same scene for our own school, Cutlers' Grammar School, Sheffield, with the boys crowding round the noticeboard and exulting in their success.

No such scene occurred in my youth as the results came by post and were slightly mysterious when they did. Whereas I had done well in the earlier exam, School Certificate, in Higher School Certificate, the equivalent of A-levels, I did well enough in History but indifferently in English and not at all well in Latin. They were just good enough, though, to get me a scholarship from Leeds City Council, but not a State Scholarship, which was thought to be superior. There was none of the over-excitement that attends the posting of such results these days, as it was easier to get to university (and to be paid for there), and so wasn't made such a fuss of as nowadays (not that there isn't anything that is not made a fuss of nowadays). I can't imagine my fellow sixth-formers behaving like ours do on film, embracing one another, jumping on each other's backs in the manner of goal-scoring footballers.

With us a gloomy satisfaction was more the order of the day; this was one examination, but there were going to be others, and more hurdles to come. And before all that the worst hurdle of all, the army.

And, of course, what nobody tells you, then or now, is that it won't matter. Nobody has ever asked me what my results were at school or since. I have never had to say what class of degree I got or even where I was educated. Did anybody go to university on the unit? Nick apart, I have no idea. But what examinations did procure was time. The vague promissory capabilities of A-levels and degrees count for very little except that they give you a breathing space. Life can be put off.

19 August Sacha Dhawan has been auditioning for one of the films being made about 9 /11. He does the speech he's been given very well, only then the director says, 'Now do it in Arabic.' Sacha is English, born and bred in Manchester, and can no more speak Arabic than he can Serbo-Croat. He points this out, whereupon an Arab speaker is procured whom Sacha is supposed to imitate. He does his best but ends up just making Arabic-type noises, at which the director professes himself well satisfied. Luvvies nothing: actors are both saints and heroes.

22 August When I ask myself why the filming has been so easy and good-tempered I think, well that's how the whole play has been, right from the start. This is partly thanks to Nick H's temperament (or lack of it) and also to the fact that we get on well.

A film, though, is different. Schedules these days are horrendously tight, with an enormous amount crammed into each day. So that even when, as with us, lighting is kept to a minimum, we're always working against the clock.

That nobody feels this particularly or gets obviously ratty is, I suspect, more down to the cameraman, Andrew Dunn, than one realises. He's quiet, shy and self-effacing and looks like a kindlier Wittgenstein. Good temper starts with him and spreads through the crew. I don't think I've ever worked on an easier, more relaxed film than this . . . and obviously there are other factors (the cast knowing the play so well, for a start) . . . but Andrew is at the centre of it.

24 August Fountains Abbey. Been here before, I keep thinking, though not just about Fountains which I've known all my life. No, it's the filming that is the same. I first filmed here in 1972 with Stephen Frears when we were making *A Day Out*. Today we set up camp with our rugs and chairs on the same spot and at one point we are waiting for the sun for a shot identical with one we framed all of thirty years ago.

I show Sam Barnett and Russell Tovey and Justine from costumes the echo under the cliff at the east end of the nave, something I put in the script of *A Day Out* and had David Waller testing out. That was the first film I ever did. Now I'm back at Fountains and maybe this will be my last film. Still, not a bad place to start and not a bad place to finish either. This time, though, we can shoot in the nave, which we couldn't then, as Abbot Huby's tower was covered in scaffolding. 'Great production values,' someone says, and so they are, particularly when we get the occasional flash of late sunshine. The film ends with Hector saying his 'Pass the parcel' speech as they all line up on the high altar for a class photograph.

1 November In the earliest draft of *The History Boys*, which we for a time rehearsed, one of the many quotations Hector bandied about (cut when it was slimmed down) was from Jowett, the nineteenth-century Master of Balliol.

'We have sought the truth, and sometimes perhaps we have found it. But have we had any *fun*?'

Well, one thing that can be said about the play and the film is, yes, we have had fun, and lots of it.

ALAN BENNETT

CAST AND CREDITS

The History Boys is a National Theatre Production and was made in association with BBC Films, Fox Searchlight Pictures, DNA Films and the UK Film Council. The cast was as follows:

HECTOR	Richard Griffiths
IRWIN	Stephen Campbell Moore
MRS LINTOTT	Frances de la Tour
HEADMASTER	Clive Merrison
POSNER	Samuel Barnett
DAKIN	Dominic Cooper
AKHTAR	Sacha Dhawan
CROWTHER	Samuel Anderson
LOCKWOOD	Andrew Knott
RUDGE	Russell Tovey
SCRIPPS	Jamie Parker
TIMMS	James Corden
FIONA	Georgia Taylor
WILKES	Adrian Scarborough
MRS BIBBY	Penelope Wilton
LOLLIPOP LADY	Maggie McCarthy
OXFORD DONS	Iain Mitchell, David Killick
JANICE	Laura Elphinstone
SLEEPING CLERGYMAN	Patrick Godfrey

Director	Nicholas Hytner
Screenplay by	Alan Bennett and Nicholas Hytner
Produced by	Kevin Loader, Nicholas Hytner, Damian Jones
Executive Producers	David M. Thompson, Andrew McDonald, Allon Reich, Charles Moore, Miles Ketley
Line Producer	Julia Stannard
Director of Photography	Andrew Dunn, BSC
Film Editor	John Wilson, ACE
Production Designer	John Beard
Costume Designer	Justine Luxton
Make-up Designer	Daniel Phillips
Music by	George Fenton
Casting Director	Toby Whale, CDG

THE HISTORY BOYS: THE FILM

*This shooting script includes some scenes
that were cut from the screenplay in the editing*

EXT. STREET. DAY.

Posner, a seventeen-year-old boy, is cycling towards school, headphones on, listening to some Ivor Novello ('I can give you the moon', say). It is summer, mid-1980s.

He stops outside a church, where there is another bike in the porch. He waits.

INT. CHURCH. DAY.

Inside the church Scripps, also seventeen or eighteen, is just taking Communion, the only other communicants a couple of old ladies. Scripps frowning in prayer.

EXT. CHURCH PORCH. DAY.

Posner waiting in the porch as Scripps comes out.

POSNER
Will that do the trick, do you think?

Scripps pulls a face and gets on his bike.

SCRIPPS
We're about to find out.

EXT. SCHOOL. DAY.

A large city grammar school in Yorkshire (boys only, ages eleven to eighteen), possibly on the outskirts of the city, with its own playing fields, tennis courts, etc.

A milk float waits outside the entrance.

Posner and Scripps cycle up as an old car pulls up. Scripps stops by the milk float, which is driven by Lockwood.

SCRIPPS

Let's get it over with.

As they go towards the school buildings Akhtar gets out of the car, which we see has his father and mother and various brothers and sisters in it too.

INT. CORRIDOR OUTSIDE HEADMASTER'S STUDY. DAY.

Various boys (and their parents) standing around, none of them in school uniform. They are all seventeen or eighteen, and they are waiting for their A-level results.

Posner, Scripps and Lockwood are joined by the other History Boys – eight of them in all. They are all very bright, with the possible exception of Rudge, who compensates for his inarticulacy by excelling on the rugby pitch. Posner is Jewish, a late developer. Scripps is a budding writer, wry and articulate. Lockwood is loud and good-natured. Joining them are Timms, who is a merciless piss-taker; Akhtar, who is seriously clever, small and bright-eyed; and Crowther – reserved and easygoing.

Fiona comes out of the headmaster's office with the list, which she pins up. She is the Headmaster's secretary, an object of almost universal desire.

Some rush but with an attempt at cool. All the Boys are pleased, with Rudge showing it less than the others. Dakin saunters up, the last of the History Boys. He is supremely self-confident, and seems to be intimate with Fiona.

SCRIPPS

Are you not going to look?

DAKIN

I got mine last night.

He smirks at Fiona.

SCRIPPS

I bet you did.

TIMMS

Jammy sod.

The Headmaster appears as Akhtar goes to tell his family.

4

HEADMASTER

Lockwood. Why are you dressed as a milkman?

LOCKWOOD

Working, sir, for the holidays.

HEADMASTER

As a milkman?

He looks pained.

After the holidays you will be coming back to try for Oxford and Cambridge. Meanwhile try and do something fitting.

POSNER

I'm in a bookshop, sir.

HEADMASTER

Good, good.

CROWTHER

I'm on the bins, sir.

TIMMS

Bouncer, sir.

AKHTAR

Lavatory attendant, sir.

DAKIN

Gigolo, sir.

The Headmaster winces and retires.

Hector has meanwhile come up behind the group at the noticeboard with Mrs Lintott. Hector is the staff-room maverick, fifty-five and portly. He teaches English. Mrs Lintott (Dorothy) is a history teacher, also in her mid-fifties.

HECTOR

Dorothy. Boys, well done! So. We shall be meeting again after all.

BOYS
(affecting resignation)

Yes, sir.

HECTOR

At school, you see, Dakin, you don't get parole. Good behaviour just brings a longer sentence. You poor boys.

The Boys disappear down the corridor. Hector looks after them.

'The happiest youth, viewing his progress through
What perils past, what crosses to ensue
Would shut the book and sit him down and die.'

Congratulations, Dorothy. You must be very pleased.

EXT. SCHOOL. DAY.

Titles and credits.

As the autumn term begins, boys of all ages arrive; teachers get out of their cars; the History Boys, now in uniform, greet each other. Hector roars through the school gates on his motorbike.

INT. MRS LINTOTT'S CLASSROOM. DAY.

The first lesson of the new term. Mrs Lintott and the eight Boys.

MRS LINTOTT

You are entitled, though only for five minutes, Dakin, to feel pleased with yourselves. No one has done as well – not in English, not in Science, not even dare I say it, in Media Studies. And you alone are up for Oxford and Cambridge. So. To work. First essay this term will be the Church on the eve of the Reformation.

TIMMS

Not again, miss.

MRS LINTOTT

This is Oxford and Cambridge. You don't just need to know it. You need to know it backwards. Facts, facts, facts.

With a groan, pulling textbooks from their bags, they set to work.

6

INT. HEADMASTER'S STUDY. DAY.

The Headmaster is talking to Mrs Lintott.

> HEADMASTER
> They're clever but they're crass, and were it Bristol or York
> I would have no worries. But Oxford and Cambridge. We need
> a strategy, Dorothy, a game plan.

> MRS LINTOTT
> They know their stuff.

> HEADMASTER
> But they lack flair. Culture they can get from Hector, and
> history from you . . . but (I'm thinking aloud now) is there
> something else . . .

> MRS LINTOTT
> Properly organised facts are . . .

> HEADMASTER
> This is Oxford and Cambridge, Dorothy. Facts are just the
> beginning.

Fiona has come in.

> Think charm. Think polish. Think Renaissance Man. Leave it
> with me, Dorothy. Leave it with me.

*He goes back to his desk and takes out Irwin's application with his
photograph from beneath his blotter.*

A knock at the door.

> Come.

Wilkes is in gym shoes, tracksuit bottoms: plainly the PE master.

> Wilkes, ah yes. An innovation to the timetable. PE.

> WILKES
> Yes, Headmaster.

> HEADMASTER
> For the Oxbridge set. Surely not, you say. But why not? This is
> the biggest hurdle of their lives and I want them galvanised.

Galvanised, yes, Headmaster.

Headmaster leads Wilkes out of the office.

EXT. SCHOOL. DAY.

HEADMASTER
Holistic . . . is that the word I'm groping for? Mind, body, body, mind. An edge to the body, an edge to the mind. Some of them smoke. They deserve to take exercise.

Headmaster jumps on a boy.

Crisps, boy, crisps. This is what we do with crisps.

He leads the boy to a bin, scrunches up the packet and chucks them away. Behind him, we see, emerging from his old car, Irwin, the supply History teacher whose application the Headmaster has earlier inspected. He is twenty-five or so.

INT. HECTOR'S CLASSROOM. DAY.

Most of the Boys' lessons will be in History, but now they are with Hector whose assignment is to prepare them for the General Studies paper that all Oxbridge entrants have to take.

HECTOR
On the timetable our esteemed Headmaster gives these periods the dubious title of General Studies. I will let you into a secret, boys. There is no such thing as General Studies. General Studies is a waste of time. Knowledge is not general. It is specific – and – (*He lowers his voice.*) – it has nothing to do with getting on.

As he talks he walks behind Posner, who looks directly at the camera, which stays with him.

POSNER
(*to camera*)
This was always Hector's way. He made learning a conspiracy, a plot between us and him. I loved it.

RUDGE
(*to Posner*)
I didn't. What was the fucking point?

HECTOR
But remember, open quotation marks, 'All knowledge is precious whether or not it serves the slightest human use,' close quotation marks.

Who said? Lockwood? Crowther? Timms? Akhtar?

Pause

'Loveliest of trees, the cherry now –'

AKHTAR
A. E. Housman, sir.

TIMMS
Wasn't he a nancy, sir?

HECTOR
Foul, festering grubby-minded little trollop. Do not use that word.

He hits him with a book.

TIMMS
You use it, sir.

HECTOR
I do, sir, I know but I am far gone in age and decrepitude.

CROWTHER
You're not supposed to hit us, sir. We could report you, sir.

HECTOR
(*despair*)
I know, I know.

An elaborate pantomime, all this.

DAKIN
Remember, sir, we're scholarship candidates now. We're all going in for Oxford and Cambridge, sir.

9

HECTOR

Oxford and Cambridge, what for?

LOCKWOOD

Old, sir. Tried and tested.

HECTOR

No, sir. It's because other boys want to go there. The hot ticket. Standing room only.

CROWTHER
(*winking*)

Where did you go, sir?

HECTOR

Sheffield. I was very happy.

'Happy is England, sweet her artless daughters.
Enough her simple loveliness for me.'

Keats.

CROWTHER

We won't be examined on that, will we, sir?

HECTOR

Keats?

CROWTHER

Happiness.

He hits them.

DAKIN

You're hitting us again, sir.

HECTOR

Child, I am your teacher. Whatever I do in this room is a token of my trust.

I am in your hands. It is a pact. Bread eaten in secret.

'I have put before you life and death, blessing and cursing; therefore choose life, that both thou and thy seed may live.' Oxford and Cambridge!

INT. CORRIDOR OUTSIDE HEADMASTER'S STUDY. DAY.

Irwin is waiting outside the study. Scripps is passing by when the Headmaster appears.

> HEADMASTER
>
> You are?

> IRWIN
>
> Irwin.

> HEADMASTER
>
> Irwin?

> IRWIN
>
> The supply teacher.

> HEADMASTER
>
> Quite so.

Scripps has watched this and turns to camera.

> SCRIPPS
>
> Hector had said that if I wanted to write I should keep a notebook and there must have been something furtive about Irwin's arrival because I wrote it down. I called it clandestine, a word I'd just learnt and wasn't sure how to pronounce.

INT. HEADMASTER'S STUDY. DAY.

Irwin is now sitting with the Headmaster.

> HEADMASTER
>
> The examinations are at the end of term, which gives us three months at the outside. Well, you were at Cambridge, you know the form.

> IRWIN
>
> Oxford, Jesus.

> HEADMASTER
>
> I thought of going, but this was the fifties. Change was in the air. A spirit of adventure.

IRWIN

So, where did you go?

HEADMASTER

I was a geographer. I went to Hull.

An awkward pause.

They are a likely lot, the boys. All keen. One oddity. Rudge.
Determined to try for Oxford, and Christ Church of all places.
No hope. Might get in at Loughborough in a bad year. Otherwise
all bright. But they need finish. Edge. Your job. We are low in the
league. I want to see us up there with Manchester Grammar
School, Haberdashers' Aske's, Leighton Park. Or is that an
open prison? No matter.

Pause.

There is a vacancy in History.

IRWIN
(*thoughtfully*)

That's very true.

HEADMASTER

In the school.

IRWIN

Ah.

HEADMASTER

Get me scholarships, Irwin, pull us up the table and it is yours.
I am corseted by the curriculum, but I can find you three
lessons a week.

IRWIN

Not enough.

Headmaster looks at the wall timetable.

HEADMASTER

Ye-es. I think I know where we can filch an hour. You are very
young. Grow a moustache. I am thinking classroom control.

INT. HECTOR'S CLASSROOM. DAY.

Posner is singing an Edith Piaf song, 'L'Accordioniste', accompanied by Scripps. Hector's disdain for anything like a curriculum is indulged by the Boys. When the song finishes –

HECTOR
Où voudriez-vous travailler cet après-midi?

Groans.

DAKIN
Je voudrais travailler . . . dans une maison de passe.

HECTOR
Oo la la.

Boys –

Qu'est-ce que c'est?

Qu'est-ce qu'une maison de passe?

POSNER
A brothel.

HECTOR
Très bien. Mais une maison de passe où tous les clients utilisent le subjonctif, ou le conditionnel, oui?

He motions to Dakin, who goes out of the classroom, and knocks on the door.

POSNER
Entrez, s'il vous plaît.

Voilà votre lit and voici votre prostituée.

Posner indicates Timms.

DAKIN
Je veux m'étendre sur le lit.

HECTOR
Je voudrais . . . I would like to stretch out on the bed in the conditional or the subjunctive. *Continuez, mes enfants.*

Dakin makes to lie down on some chairs.

POSNER

Mais les chaussures, monsieur, pas sur le lit.

DAKIN

Excusez moi, Mademoiselle.

POSNER

Et votre pantalon s'il vous plaît.

Dakin takes off trousers.

Oh. Quelles belles jambes.

Dakin examines his own legs with approval.

Et maintenant . . . Claudine.

Timms does a passable impression of Catherine Deneuve.

DAKIN

Oui, la prostituée, s'il vous plaît.

CLAUDINE (TIMMS)

A quel prix?

DAKIN

Dix francs.

CLAUDINE

Pour dix francs je peux vous montrer ma prodigieuse poitrine.

There is a knock at the door.

POSNER

Un autre client.

Posner opens the door. The Boys freeze in horror. Hector is unperturbed.

HECTOR

Ah, cher Monsieur le Directeur –

The Headmaster comes in with Irwin. Dakin stands trouserless in front of them.

HEADMASTER

Mr Hector, what on earth is happening . . .

Hector holds up an admonitory finger.

HECTOR

L'anglais, c'est interdit. Ici on ne parle que français, en accordant une importance particulière au subjonctif.

The Headmaster is cornered.

HEADMASTER

Oh, ah.

Et qu'est-ce qui se passe ici?

Pourquoi cet garçon . . . Dakin isn't it? . . . est sans ses . . . trousers?

HECTOR

Quelqu'un? Ne sois pas timide. Dites à cher Monsieur le Directeur ce que nous faisons.

The Boys are frozen. Hector beams at them.

DAKIN

Je suis un homme qui . . .

HECTOR

Vous n'êtes pas un homme. Vous êtes un soldat . . . un soldat blessé, vous comprenez cher Monsieur le Directeur . . . soldat blessé?

HEADMASTER

Wounded soldier, of course, yes.

HECTOR

Ici c'est un hôpital en Belgique.

HEADMASTER

Belgique? Pourquoi Belgique?

AKHTAR

Ypres, sir. Ypres. *Pendant la Guerre Mondiale Numéro Un.*

HECTOR

C'est ça. Dakin est un soldat blessé, un mutilé de guerre et les autres sont des médecins, infirmiéres et tout le personnel d'un grand établissement médical et thérapeutique.

Continuez, mes enfants.

HEADMASTER

Mais . . .

Lockwood begins to moan. The others follow suit. Screams, groans, an over-the-top portrayal of a field hospital.

AKHTAR

Qu'il souffre!

HECTOR

Il est distrait.

IRWIN

Il est commotionné, peut être?

HECTOR

Comment?

IRWIN

Commotionné. Shell-shocked.

There is a perceptible moment.

HECTOR

C'est possible. Commotionné. Oui, c'est le mot juste.

HEADMASTER

Permettez-moi d'introduire M. Irwin, notre nouveau professeur.

HECTOR

Enchanté.

HEADMASTER

Enough of this . . . silliness. Not silliness, no . . . but . . . Mr Hector, you are aware that these pupils are Oxbridge candidates.

HECTOR

Are they? Are you sure? Nobody has told me.

HEADMASTER

Mr Irwin will be coaching them, but it's a question of time. I have found him three lessons a week and I was wondering . . .

HECTOR

No, Headmaster. (*He covers his ears.*)

HEADMASTER

Purely on a temporary basis. It will be the last time, I promise.

HECTOR

Last time was the last time also.

HEADMASTER

I am thinking of the boys.

HECTOR

I, too. *Non. Absolument non. Non. Non. Non. C'est hors de question. Et puis, si vous voulez m'excuser, je dois continuer le leçon. À tout à l'heure.*

Headmaster looks at Irwin.

HEADMASTER

Fuck.

They go as the bell goes. Hector picks up helmet.

RUDGE

It's true, though, sir. We don't have much time.

AKHTAR

We don't even have to do French.

HECTOR

Now, who goes home?

There are no offers.

Surely I can give someone a lift?

Who's on pillion duty?

Dakin?

DAKIN

Not me, sir. Going into town.

HECTOR

Crowther?

CROWTHER

Off for a run, sir.

HECTOR

Akhtar?

AKHTAR

Computer club, sir.

POSNER

I'll come, sir.

HECTOR

No. No. Never mind.

SCRIPPS
(*resignedly*)

I'll come, sir.

HECTOR

Ah, Scripps.

SCRIPPS

The things I do for Jesus.

Hector and Scripps go.

POSNER

It's never me.

LOCKWOOD

You're too young, still.

DAKIN

Though it will happen. Now that you have achieved puberty . . .

LOCKWOOD

If rather late in the day . . .

DAKIN

Mr Hector is likely at some point to put his hand on your knee. This is because Mr Hector is a homosexual and a sad fuck. The drill is to look at the hand and say, 'And what does Mr Hector want?' He has no answer to this and so will desist.

EXT. SCHOOL CAR PARK. DAY.

> HECTOR
> (*crash-helmeted and on the bike*).

Thrutch up.

Scripps, also in helmet and on the pillion, grips Hector tighter. They roar off.

EXT. STREET. DAY.

They pass a woman, who notices something and looks back.

EXT. ROAD. DAY.

The bike cruises along. Scripps' patient, bored face, hands on his helmeted head.

INT. SCHOOL CORRIDOR. DAY.

Mrs Lintott and the Headmaster.

> MRS LINTOTT
> I just think I should have been told.

> HEADMASTER
> He comes highly recommended.

> MRS LINTOTT
> So did Anne of Cleves.

> HEADMASTER
> Who? He's up-to-the-minute, Dorothy. More *now*.

> MRS LINTOTT
> Now? I thought history was *then*.

INT. CANTEEN. DAY.

Headmaster approaches Akhtar and Timms as they queue for lunch.

> HEADMASTER
> Anne of Cleves? Remind me.

AKHTAR

Fourth wife of Henry VIII, sir.

HEADMASTER

Of course.

TIMMS

She was the one they told him was Miss Dish, only when she
turned up she had a face like the wrong end of a camel's turd.

HEADMASTER

Quite so.

INT. HEADMASTER'S STUDY. DAY.

*After his rebuff in the French class, the Headmaster is scanning the
timetable. Irwin stands waiting.*

HEADMASTER

Fiona!

She comes in.

INT. CHANGING ROOMS. DAY.

Class of around twenty-five or so, including the History Boys.

TIMMS

I've brought a note, sir.

WILKES

How much for?

I don't do notes. Get changed.

TIMMS

Sir . . .

WILKES

God doesn't do notes either. Did Jesus say, 'Can I be excused
the crucifixion?'

No.

Actually, sir, I think he did.

WILKES

Change.

INT. GYMNASIUM. DAY.

Posner is struggling on the wall-bars.

WILKES

Frame yourself, boy. Oxford and Cambridge won't want a boy that can't hang upside down on the wall-bars.

After some failure to get over the horse or whatever.

You're letting yourself down. You're letting God down.

LOCKWOOD

What's God got to do with it?

WILKES

Listen, boy. This isn't your body.

LOCKWOOD

No?

WILKES

This body is on loan to you from God.

LOCKWOOD

Fuck me.

WILKES

I heard that. Give me five.

LOCKWOOD

Five what? Hail Marys?

WILKES

Do it.

He is doing them when Irwin's shoes come into shot.

You're late.

Get your kit off.

IRWIN

I'm on the staff.

WILKES

I've never seen you. What's this?

Irwin hands him a note, which he studies.

TIMMS

Do you want any help, sir?

AKHTAR

Is it joined-up writing?

Wilkes fumes and then begins to read out the names of the History Boys.

INT. IRWIN'S CLASSROOM. DAY.

Irwin waiting. The Boys struggle in, some still half-dressed.

LOCKWOOD

That was ace, sir.

SCRIPPS

Yeah. Great stuff.

IRWIN

Don't thank me. Thank the Headmaster, or his secretary. Mrs Lintott has given me a sight of your latest essays. The experience was interesting, the essays not.

Irwin has a pile of the History Boys' essays. He distributes them.

Dull.

Dull.

Abysmally dull.

A triumph . . . the dullest of the lot.

DAKIN

I got all the points.

IRWIN

I didn't say it was wrong. I said it was dull. Its sheer competence was staggering.

DAKIN

Actually, sir, I know tradition requires it of the eccentric schoolmaster, but do you mind not throwing the books? They tend to fall apart.

Irwin regards them for a moment or two in silence.

IRWIN

At the time of the Reformation there were fourteen foreskins of Christ preserved, but it was thought that the church of St John Lateran in Rome had the authentic prepuce.

DAKIN

Don't think we're shocked by your mention of the word foreskin, sir.

CROWTHER

No, sir. Some of us even have them.

LOCKWOOD

Not Posner, though, sir. Posner's like, you know, Jewish.

It's one of several things Posner doesn't have.

Posner mouths 'Fuck off.'

That's not racist, though, sir.

CROWTHER

Isn't it?

LOCKWOOD

It's race-related, but it's not racist.

Another pause while Irwin regards the class.

IRWIN

Has anybody been to Rome? Venice? Florence? Well, the other candidates will have been and done courses on it, most likely, so when they get an essay like this on the Church at the time of the Reformation they will know that some silly nonsense on the foreskins of Christ will come in handy so that their essays, unlike yours, will not be dull. They're not even bad. They're just boring. You haven't got a hope.

CROWTHER

So why are we bothering?

IRWIN

You tell me. You want it. Your parents want it. Me, I'd go to Newcastle and be happy.

Long pause.

Of course, there is another way.

CROWTHER

How?

TIMMS

Cheat?

IRWIN

Possibly. And Dakin . . .?

DAKIN

Yes, sir?

IRWIN

Don't take the piss.

There isn't time.

INT. HISTORY CORRIDOR, LOCKER AREA. DAY.

They are leaving school for the day.

TIMMS

What a wanker.

DAKIN

They all have to do it, don't they?

CROWTHER

Do what?

DAKIN

Show you they're still in the game. Foreskins and stuff. Sir, you devil!

SCRIPPS

Have a heart. He's only five minutes older than we are.

DAKIN

What happened with Hector on the bike?

SCRIPPS

As per. (*He demonstrates.*) I think he thought he'd got me going. In fact it was my *Tudor Economic Documents, Volume Two*.

They stop talking as Posner comes up.

POSNER
(*to camera*)

Because I was late growing up I am not included in this kind of conversation. I'm not that sort of boy. That's probably why I'm clever.

INT. SCHOOL LIBRARY. DAY.

A montage, to music, of all the Boys feverishly studying, taking books from the shelves, books particularly about the First World War.

EXT. PLAYING FIELDS. DAY.

Rudge teeing up a rugger ball then addressing the camera before kicking a perfect goal.

RUDGE

Nobody thinks I have a hope in this exam. Well, fuck 'em.

EXT. SCHOOL GROUNDS. DAY.

Irwin and his class are sitting outside in the sun.

IRWIN

So, let's summarise. The First World War. What points do we make?

CROWTHER

Trench warfare.

LOCKWOOD

Mountains of dead.

POSNER

On both sides.

DAKIN

Generals stupid.

POSNER

On both sides.

AKHTAR

Armistice. Germany humiliated.

IRWIN

Keep it coming.

CROWTHER

Mass unemployment.

AKHTAR

Inflation.

TIMMS

Collapse of the Weimar Republic. Internal disorder and the rise of Hitler.

IRWIN

So. Our overall conclusion is that the origins of the Second War lie in the unsatisfactory outcome of the First.

TIMMS

Yes. (*Doubtfully.*) Yes. (*As they make to leave.*)

Others nod.

IRWIN

First class. Bristol welcomes you with open arms. Manchester longs to have you. You can walk into Leeds. But I am a fellow of Magdalen College, Oxford and I have just read seventy papers all saying the same thing and I am asleep . . .

SCRIPPS

But it's all true.

IRWIN

What's truth got to do with it?

What's truth got to do with anything?

INT. MRS LINTOTT'S CLASSROOM. DAY.

Hector and Mrs Lintott are watching Irwin and his class from a window.

MRS LINTOTT

The new man seems clever.

HECTOR

He does. Depressingly so.

MRS LINTOTT

Men are at history, of course.

HECTOR

Why history particularly?

MRS LINTOTT

Storytelling, so much of it, which is what men do naturally.

HECTOR

Dakin's a good-looking boy, though somehow sad.

MRS LINTOTT

You always think they're sad, Hector, every, every time.
Actually, I wouldn't have said he was sad. I would have said
he was cunt-struck.

HECTOR

Dorothy.

MRS LINTOTT

I'd have thought you'd have liked that. It's a compound
adjective. You like compound adjectives.

Oh. Going walkabout.

Irwin and his class have taken off and he is leading them out of the school.

EXT. MUNICIPAL PARK / WAR MEMORIAL. DAY.

They are walking through a municipal park.

IRWIN

The truth was, in 1914 Germany does now want war. Yes, there is an arms race, but it is Britain who is leading it. (*He stops.*) Why does no one admit this?

They turn the corner and see the war memorial.

That's why. The dead. The body count. We don't like to admit the war was even partly our fault because so many of our people died. And all the mourning has veiled the truth. It's not lest we forget, but lest we remember. That's what this is about . . . the memorials, the Cenotaph, the Two Minutes' Silence. Because there's no better way of forgetting something than by commemorating it.

He turns to Scripps.

And as for the truth, Scripps, which you were worrying about, forget it. In an examination, truth is not at issue.

DAKIN

Do you really believe that, sir, or are you just trying to make us think?

SCRIPPS

You can't explain away the poetry, sir.

LOCKWOOD

No, sir. Art wins in the end.

SCRIPPS

What about this, sir?

'Those long uneven lines
Standing as patiently
As if they were stretched outside
The Oval or Villa Park,
The crowns of hats, the sun
On moustached archaic faces
Grinning as if it were all
An August Bank Holiday lark . . .

The others take up the lines of Larkin's poem, maybe saying a couple of lines each through to the end, as they go – but matter of factly.

LOCKWOOD

'Never such innocence,
Never before or since,
As changed itself to past
Without a word –

AKHTAR

'– the men
Leaving the gardens tidy,

POSNER

'The thousands of marriages
Lasting a little while longer:

TIMMS

'Never such innocence again.'

IRWIN

How come you know all this by heart? (*Baffled, shouts.*) Not that it answers the question.

EXT. BUS STOP. DAY.

Scripps, Posner and Dakin are waiting for a bus.

SCRIPPS

So much for our glorious dead.

DAKIN

Quite. Actually, Fiona's my Western Front. Last night, for instance, I thought it might be the big push so, encountering only token resistance, I reconnoitred the ground as far as the actual place.

SCRIPPS

Shit.

DAKIN

I mean, not onto it and certainly not into it. But up to it.

Cut to:

INT. A BEDROOM. NIGHT.

Dakin and Fiona snogging, Dakin rummaging.

> DAKIN
> (*voice-over*)

The beauty of it is, the metaphor really fits. I mean, moving up to the front you presumably had to pass the sites of previous battles, like her tits, which actually only surrendered about three weeks ago, but to which I now have immediate access and which were indeed the start line for a determined thrust southwards.

What's the matter?

> FIONA
> (*signifying it's over*)

No man's land.

> DAKIN

Aw, fuck. So what do I do with this?

> FIONA
> (*sweetly*)

Carry out a controlled explosion?

Cut to:

INT./EXT. BUS. DAY.

Scripps, Posner and Dakin are on the top deck of the bus home.

> DAKIN

Still, at least I'm doing better than Felix.

> POSNER

Felix?

> SCRIPPS

No!

> DAKIN

Tries to.

POSNER

Actually, the metaphor isn't exact. Because what Fiona is presumably carrying out is a planned withdrawal. You're not forcing her. She's not being overwhelmed by superior forces. Does she like you?

DAKIN

Course she likes me.

POSNER

Then you're not disputing the territory. You're just negotiating over the pace of the occupation.

SCRIPPS

Just let us know when you get to Berlin.

DAKIN

I'm beginning to like him more.

POSNER

Who? Me?

DAKIN

Irwin. Though he hates me.

Dakin gets off the bus.

SCRIPPS

Cheer up. At least he speaks to you. Most guys wouldn't even speak to you. Love can be very irritating.

POSNER

How do you know?

SCRIPPS

It's what I always think about God. He must get so pissed off, everybody adoring him all the time.

POSNER

Yes, only you don't catch God poncing about in his underpants.

Posner looks out of the window: Dakin is walking up the street with Fiona. Posner looks miserably after them, as, in voice-over, he sings the first verse of Rodgers and Hart's 'Bewitched'.

Posner, accompanied by Scripps, is singing 'Bewitched' to Dakin. General discontent at the music and at the waste of time.

> HECTOR

Well done, Posner. Anybody know who it's by?

> CROWTHER

Who cares?

> POSNER

Rodgers and Hart, sir.

> HECTOR

And sung best by?

> CROWTHER

Oh, for Christ's sake.

> POSNER

Ella Fitzgerald.

> HECTOR

That was the lyric. Now for poetry of a more traditional sort.

Timms groans.

What is this?

> TIMMS

Sir. I don't always understand poetry.

> HECTOR

You don't always understand it? Timms, I never understand it. But learn it now, know it now and you'll understand it whenever.

> TIMMS

I don't see how we can understand it. Most of the stuff poetry's about hasn't happened to us yet.

> HECTOR

But it will, Timms. It will. And then you will have the antidote ready! Grief. Happiness. Even when you're dying. Smile! We're making your deathbeds here, boys.

LOCKWOOD

Fucking Ada!

TIMMS

But we've got an ending, sir.

HECTOR

Really? Well, be sharp! Fetch the tin.

General relief. Someone takes a large tin down from a shelf. Timms and Lockwood are at the front of the class.

TIMMS

We have to smoke, sir.

LOCKWOOD

I happen to have one, sir.

HECTOR

Very well.

Timms and Lockwood suddenly snap into an elaborate charade, both making startlingly effective jobs of assuming the voices and postures of the actors from Hollywood's golden age (another of Hector's enthusiasms).

TIMMS

Gerry, please help me.

LOCKWOOD

Shall we just have a cigarette on it?

TIMMS

Yes.

LOCKWOOD

May I sometimes come here?

TIMMS

Whenever you like. It's your home, too. There are people here who love you.

LOCKWOOD

And will you be happy, Charlotte?

TIMMS

Oh Gerry. Don't let's ask for the moon. We have the stars.

Hector pretends puzzlement, looks in the tin to count the kitty. It's clear what the game is: if he can't identify the movie, the kitty goes to the Boys.

HECTOR

Could it be Paul Henreid and Bette Davis in *Now, Voyager*?

TIMMS

Aw, sir.

HECTOR

It's famous, you ignorant little tarts.

LOCKWOOD

We'd never heard of it, sir.

HECTOR

Walt Whitman. *Leaves of Grass.*

'The untold want, by life and land ne'er granted,
Now, Voyager, sail thou forth, to seek and find.'

Fifty p. Pay up.

LOCKWOOD

Shit.

Lockwood and Timms pay up.

INT. SCHOOL LIBRARY. DAY.

Rudge is looking through the books on film. Mrs Lintott appears behind him.

RUDGE

There's nothing on the *Carry On* films.

MRS LINTOTT

Why should there be?

RUDGE

The exam. Mr Irwin said the *Carry On*s would be good films to talk about.

MRS LINTOTT

Really? How peculiar. Does he like them, do you think?

RUDGE

Probably not, miss. You never know with him.

MRS LINTOTT

I'm now wondering if there's something there that I've missed.

RUDGE

Mr Irwin says that, 'While they have no intrinsic artistic merit – (*He is reading from his notes.*) – they achieve some of the permanence of art simply by persisting and acquire an incremental significance if only as social history.'

MRS LINTOTT

Dear me. What fun you must all have.

RUDGE

It's not like your stuff, miss, it's cutting-edge. It really is.

MRS LINTOTT

Can I say something to you?

RUDGE

Miss?

MRS LINTOTT

Other people have lives. That's what education is about.

RUDGE

If you say so, miss.

INT. HISTORY CORRIDOR. DAY.

The Boys and Irwin are heading for the classroom.

TIMMS

Where do you live, sir?

IRWIN

Horsforth.

DAKIN

Oh. Not far from Mr Hector, sir. He might even give you a lift if you asked him.

It's not a loft, is it, sir?

Do you exist on an unhealthy diet of takeaway food, sir, or do
you whisk up gourmet meals for one?

Or is it a lonely pizza, sir?

INT. IRWIN'S CLASSROOM. DAY.

IRWIN

I manage. No questions from you, Dakin?

DAKIN

What they want to know, sir, is 'Do you have a life?' Or are
we it?

Are we your life?

IRWIN

Pretty dismal if you are. Because these are as – (*Giving out
books.*) – dreary as ever. You get a question, you know the
answer – but so does everyone else. So say something different,
say the opposite. Take Stalin. Generally agreed to be a monster,
and rightly. So dissent. Find something, anything, to say in his
defence.

SCRIPPS
(*to camera*)

When Irwin became well-known as a TV historian this was
his technique . . . find an assumption, then turn it on its head.
Those who were caught napping at Pearl Harbour were the
Japanese, the real culprit was President Roosevelt. Find a
proposition, invert it, then look round for proof . . . the
technique was as formal as the disciplines of the medieval
schoolmen.

IRWIN

A question is about what you know, not about what you don't
know. A question about Rembrandt, for instance, might prompt
an answer about Degas.

RUDGE
Is Degas an Old Master, sir?

TIMMS
About suffering, they were never wrong, sir. The Old Masters.
How it takes place while someone is eating or opening a
window.

IRWIN
Have you done that with Mr Hector?

TIMMS
Done what, sir?

IRWIN
The poem. You were quoting somebody. Auden.

TIMMS
Was I, sir? Sometimes it just flows out. Brims over.

IRWIN
Why does he lock the door?

They turn to each other in mock surprise.

AKHTAR
Lock the door? Does he lock the door?

IRWIN
Does he have a programme? Or is it just at random?

AKHTAR
It's just knowledge, sir.

TIMMS
The pursuit of it for its own sake, sir.

AKHTAR
Breaking bread with the dead, sir. That's what we do.

LOCKWOOD
It's higher than your stuff, sir. Nobler.

POSNER
Only not useful, sir. Mr Hector's not as focused.

TIMMS

No, not focused at all, sir. Blurred, sir, more.

AKHTAR

You're much more focused, sir.

CROWTHER

And we know what we're doing with you, sir. Half the time with him we don't know what we're doing at all. (*He mimes being mystified.*)

TIMMS

We're poor little sheep that have lost our way, sir. Where are we?

AKHTAR

You're very young, sir. This isn't your gap year, is it, sir?

IRWIN

I wish it was.

LOCKWOOD

Why, sir? Do you not like teaching us, sir? We're not just a hiccup between the end of university and the beginning of life, like Auden, are we, sir?

Dakin has been silent till now. He suddenly joins in.

DAKIN

Do you like Auden's poetry, sir?

IRWIN

Some.

DAKIN

Mr Hector does. We know about Auden. He was a schoolmaster for a bit.

IRWIN

I believe he was, yes.

DAKIN

He was. Do you think he was more like you or more like Mr Hector?

IRWIN

I've no idea. Why should he be like either of us?

DAKIN

I think he was more like Mr Hector.

A bit of a shambles. He snogged his pupils. Auden, sir. Not
Mr Hector.

IRWIN

You know more about him than I do.

DAKIN

'Lay your sleeping head, my love,
Human on my faithless arm.'

That was a pupil, sir. Shocking, isn't it?

IRWIN

So you could answer a question on Auden, then?

VARIOUS BOYS

How, sir?

No, sir.

That's in the exam, sir.

TIMMS

Mr Hector's stuff's not meant for the exam, sir. It's to make us
more rounded human beings.

IRWIN

Listen. Don't piss on your chips. This examination will be
about everything and anything you know and are. If there's
a question about Auden or whoever and you know about it,
you must answer it.

AKHTAR

We couldn't do that, sir.

That would be a betrayal of trust.

LOCKWOOD

Is nothing sacred, sir?

We're shocked.

POSNER

I would. Sir. And they would. They're taking the piss.

LOCKWOOD

'England, you have been here too long
And the songs you sing are the songs you sung
On a braver day. Now they are wrong.'

IRWIN

Who's that?

LOCKWOOD

Don't you know, sir?

IRWIN

No.

LOCKWOOD

Sir! It's Stevie Smith, sir. Of 'Not Waving but Drowning' fame.

IRWIN

Well, don't tell me that is useless knowledge. You get an essay
on post-imperial decline, losing an empire and finding a role,
all that stuff, and a gobbet like that is the perfect way to end it.

LOCKWOOD

A what, sir?

IRWIN

A gobbet, a quotation. How much more stuff like that have you
got up your sleeves?

LOCKWOOD

We've got all sorts, sir. The train! The train!

*And immediately Posner and Scripps are on their feet. Posner is an
uncannily accurate Celia Johnson, Scripps a tight-lipped Cyril Raymond.
Scripps even manages to play Rachmaninov to accompany the first part of
the scene.*

POSNER (CELIA JOHNSON)

I really meant to do it. I stood there right on the edge. But I
couldn't. I wasn't brave enough. I would like to be able to say
it was the thought of you and the children that prevented me
but it wasn't.

I had no thoughts at all.

Only an overwhelming desire not to feel anything at all ever again.

Not to be unhappy any more.

I went back into the refreshment room. That's when I nearly fainted.

IRWIN

What is all this?

SCRIPPS (CYRIL RAYMOND)

Laura.

POSNER (CELIA JOHNSON)

Yes, dear.

SCRIPPS (CYRIL RAYMOND)

Whatever your dream was, it wasn't a very happy one, was it?

POSNER (CELIA JOHNSON)

No.

SCRIPPS (CYRIL RAYMOND)

Is there anything I can do to help?

POSNER (CELIA JOHNSON)

You always help, dear.

SCRIPPS (CYRIL RAYMOND)

You've been a long way away.

Thank you for coming back to me.

She cries and he embraces her.

IRWIN

God knows why you've learned *Brief Encounter*.

The Boys applaud fulsomely.

BOYS

Oh very good, sir. Full marks sir.

IRWIN

But I think you ought to know this lesson has been a complete waste of time.

DAKIN

Like Mr Hector's lessons then, sir. They're a waste of time, too.

IRWIN

Yes, you little smartarse, but he's not trying to get you through an exam.

INT. STAFF ROOM. DAY.

Hector, who has been sitting reading a racing paper, gets up to leave and on his way whispers to Wilkes, who is pinning up a NO SMOKING *notice.*

HECTOR

French Kiss?

WILKES

I beg your pardon?

HECTOR

Three o'clock at Chepstow.

Hector leaves. Mrs Lintott and Irwin are at the tea trolley.

MRS LINTOTT

How're you finding them?

Irwin shrugs.

IRWIN

You've taught them too well. They can't see it's a game.

MRS LINTOTT

History? Is it a game?

IRWIN

For an exam like this, yes.

She is lighting up.

WILKES

Dorothy.

He indicates the notice.

MRS LINTOTT

Fuck.

She and Irwin leave, passing the Headmaster as they are going out.

INT. CORRIDOR. DAY.

They are on their way out.

> MRS LINTOTT
> (*of the Headmaster*)
> I call him the Awful Warning. If you don't watch out he's what
> you turn into. If this were a film in the forties he'd be played by
> Raymond Huntley.

> IRWIN
> Who?

> MRS LINTOTT
> He made a speciality of sour-faced judges and vinegary
> schoolmasters.

> IRWIN
> Who would I be played by?

> MRS LINTOTT
> Dirk Bogarde?

> IRWIN
> I'm not sure I like that.

*As they turn the corner, Hector comes down the corridor. Mrs Bibby, the
art teacher, stops him.*

> MRS BIBBY
> Hector: the very man!

> HECTOR
> Oh, stink. Hello, Hazel.

> MRS BIBBY
> Our lord and master having grudgingly conceded that art may
> have its uses, I gather I am supposed to give your Oxford and
> Cambridge boys a smattering of art history.

> HECTOR
> Not my bag, Hazel. Irwin's your man.

> IRWIN
> (*heading off*)
>
> It's really just the icing on the cake.

> MRS BIBBY
>
> Was art ever anything else?

She hurries away down the corridor.

INT. ART ROOM. DAY.

The Boys are examining art books. Mrs Bibby sees Timms with Michelangelo.

> MRS BIBBY
>
> Michelangelo. We-ell. I suppose.

> TIMMS
> (*to Akhtar*)
>
> Who've you got?

Akhtar shows him Caravaggio.

> Both nancies.

> AKHTAR
>
> Are they?

> TIMMS
>
> Well, these aren't women.

He shows him the Michelangelo.

> They're just men with tits. And the tits look as if they've been put on with an ice-cream scoop.

Back at the tables Mrs Bibby is with Lockwood.

> MRS BIBBY
>
> Do you like Turner, then?

> LOCKWOOD
>
> They're all right.

> MRS BIBBY
>
> Well, choose somebody you do like. Art is meant to be enjoyed.

In the long term, miss, maybe. But with us, enjoyment doesn't come into it. We haven't got time to read the books. We haven't got time to look at the pictures. What we really want is lessons in acting, because that's what this whole scholarship thing is . . . an acting job.

All the Boys are gone. Mrs Bibby is talking to herself pretty much, as she shelves some books.

MRS BIBBY

The best way to teach art would be to ban it. Put it out of bounds. That way they'd be sneaking in here all the time. Art is furtive, unofficial; it's something on the side.

She puts a bowl of hyacinths back on the table.

The mistake is to put it on the syllabus. Yes, Hazel, thank you very much.

EXT. SCHOOL GROUNDS. DAY.

Mrs Lintott and Irwin outside, smoking at last.

MRS LINTOTT

So have the boys given you a nickname?

IRWIN

Not that I'm aware of.

MRS LINTOTT

A nickname is an achievement . . . both in the sense of something won and also in its armorial sense of a badge, a blazon. Unsurprisingly I am Tot or Totty. Some irony there, one feels.

IRWIN

Hector has no nickname.

MRS LINTOTT

Yes he has. Hector.

IRWIN

But he's called Hector.

MRS LINTOTT

And that's his nickname too. He isn't called Hector. His name's Douglas, though the only person I've ever heard address him as such is his somewhat unexpected wife.

In the distance, Dakin and Scripps are out for a run. Irwin is reminded of something.

IRWIN

Posner came to see me yesterday. He has a problem.

MRS LINTOTT

No nickname, but at least you get their problems. I seldom do.

INT. IRWIN'S CLASSROOM. DAY.

Posner and Irwin are alone in the classroom.

POSNER

Sir, I think I may be homosexual.

EXT. SCHOOL GROUNDS. DAY.

IRWIN

'Posner,' I wanted to say, 'you are not yet in a position to be anything.'

MRS LINTOTT

You're young, of course. I never had that advantage.

INT. IRWIN'S CLASSROOM. DAY.

POSNER

I love Dakin.

IRWIN

Does Dakin know?

POSNER

Yes. He doesn't think it's surprising. Though Dakin likes girls basically.

EXT. SCHOOL GROUNDS. DAY.

> IRWIN

I sympathised, though not so much as to suggest I might be in the same boat.

> MRS LINTOTT

With Dakin?

> IRWIN

With anybody.

Maybe Irwin has been looking at Dakin, still running with Scripps.

> MRS LINTOTT

That's sensible. One of the hardest things for boys to learn is that a teacher is human. One of the hardest things for a teacher to learn is not to try and tell them.

INT. IRWIN'S CLASSROOM. DAY.

> POSNER

Is it a phase, sir?

> IRWIN

Do you think it's a phase?

> POSNER

Some of the literature says it will pass.

> IRWIN
> (*voice-over*)

I wanted to say that the literature may say that, but that literature doesn't.

> POSNER

I'm not sure I want it to pass.

But I want to get into Cambridge, sir. If I do, Dakin might love me.

Or I might stop caring. Do you look at your life, sir?

> IRWIN

I thought everyone did.

POSNER

I'm a Jew.

I'm small.

I'm homosexual.

And I live in Sheffield.

I'm fucked.

EXT. SCHOOL GROUNDS. DAY.

MRS LINTOTT

Did you let that go?

IRWIN

'Fucked'? Yes, I did, I'm afraid.

MRS LINTOTT

It's a test. A way of finding out if you've ceased to be a teacher
and become a friend. He's a bright boy. You'll see. Next time
he'll go further. What else did you talk about?

IRWIN

Nothing. No. Nothing.

She goes back inside.

INT. IRWIN'S CLASSROOM. DAY.

IRWIN

Posner? Why didn't you ask Mr Hector about Dakin?

Pause.

POSNER

I wanted advice, sir. Mr Hector would just have given me a
quotation. Housman, sir, probably. Literature is medicine,
wisdom, elastoplast. Everything. It isn't, though, is it, sir?

IRWIN

It will pass.

POSNER

Will it, sir? How do you know?

48

EXT. SCHOOL GROUNDS. DAY.

Dakin and Scripps finish their run. Dakin waves at Irwin. Irwin goes.

INT. CHANGING ROOMS. DAY.

They are changing.

> DAKIN
> So all this religion, what do you do?

> SCRIPPS
> Go to church. Pray.

> DAKIN
> Yes?

> SCRIPPS
> It's so time-consuming. You've no idea.

> DAKIN
> What else?

> SCRIPPS
> It's what you don't do.

> DAKIN
> You don't not wank? Jesus. You're headed for the bin.

> SCRIPPS
> It's not for ever.

> DAKIN
> Yeah? Just tell me on the big day and I'll stand well back.

INT. CHANGING ROOMS. DAY — A LITTLE LATER.

Dakin is fixing his hair, or whatever.

> DAKIN
> What bothers me, though, is the more you read the more you
> see that literature is about losers.

> SCRIPPS
> No.

49

DAKIN

It is. Consolation. All literature is consolation.

I don't care what Hector says, I find literature really lowering.

SCRIPPS

This is Irwin, isn't it? A line of stuff for the exam.

DAKIN

No.

As they make to leave, he takes a book from his sports bag.

Actually it isn't wholly my idea.

I've been reading this book by Kneeshaw.

SCRIPPS

Who?

DAKIN
(*shows him book*)

Kneeshaw. He's a philosopher. Frederick Kneeshaw.

SCRIPPS

I think that's pronounced Nietzsche.

DAKIN

Shit. Shit. Shit.

INT. CORRIDOR OUTSIDE HEADMASTER'S STUDY. DAY.

Dakin still furious as they pass Fiona.

SCRIPPS

What's the matter?

DAKIN

I talked to Irwin about it. He didn't correct me. He let me call him Kneeshaw. He'll think I'm a right fool. Shit.

FIONA

What have I done?

DAKIN

Nothing. You have done nothing. The world doesn't revolve around you, you know.

Dakin goes angrily into the classroom, as Irwin turns the corner, bumping into the Headmaster.

HEADMASTER

How are our young men doing? Are they 'on stream'?

IRWIN

I think so.

HEADMASTER

You think so? Are they or aren't they?

IRWIN

It must always be something of a lottery.

HEADMASTER

A lottery? I don't like the sound of that. Irwin. I don't want you to fuck up. We have been down that road too many times before.

EXT. ROAD NEAR THE SCHOOL. DAY.

Hector and Dakin on the motorbike, Hector with his hand behind him. A Lollipop Lady steps out and stops the traffic. Hector stops the bike (with both hands) but then attempts to rest his hand back on Dakin's bored crotch. Hector never gets very far, and none of the Boys who accept lifts from him seem remotely bothered by his helpless fumbling on their thighs.

The Lollipop Lady, ferrying children across the road, sees this.

Coming back across the road she has a second look. Hector's hand is still where it was.

Dakin taps Hector on the shoulder, indicating he can go. Hector zooms off, the Lollipop Lady looking at the number plate.

EXT. SCHOOL. DAY.

A minibus waiting. Irwin counting the class in.

Mrs Lintott comes out and gets in.

MRS LINTOTT

He's coming.

Cut to:

INT. CORRIDOR OUTSIDE HEADMASTER'S STUDY. DAY.

Hector with his picnic basket, hurrying along the corridor past the Headmaster's study door.

There is a lollipop sign leaning against the wall by the study door.

EXT. SCHOOL. DAY.

Hector gets in a minibus with Irwin, Mrs Lintott and the Boys. It leaves the school.

EXT. RUINS OF FOUNTAINS ABBEY. DAY.

Minibus parked. Irwin with some Boys striding through. Hector and Mrs Lintott idly strolling about.

> IRWIN
> They took the lead off the roofs, used the timbers to melt it down and time did the rest. All thanks to Henry VIII. If you want to learn about Stalin, study Henry VIII. If you want to learn about Mrs Thatcher, study Henry VIII. If you want to learn about Hollywood, study Henry VIII.

> HECTOR
> While you and Dorothy are taking them through the history, I'll pitch camp here.

He settles down.

> Though, Irwin, I am available in a consultative capacity for the provision of useful quotations. 'Gobbets – (*He bows to Irwin.*) – on request.' 'Bare ruin'd choirs where late the sweet birds sang.'

Irwin and the Boys go on as Hector shouts after them.

> Remember, boys. Festoon your answers with 'gobbets' and you won't go far wrong.

> IRWIN
> (*to the Boys and a bored Mrs Lintott*)
> Actually, singing was the least of it. The monks were farmers,

clothiers, tanners, tailors. They mined for lead. They were captains of industry.

EXT. RUINS OF ABBEY. A DITCH. DAY.

TIMMS

This was the shithouse.

IRWIN

No, Timms, up there was the shithouse. This was the drain.

CROWTHER

They sat up there and the stuff dropped down here?

TIMMS

Bit draughty on the bum, sir.

AKHTAR

This wasn't a thoroughfare was it, sir?

IRWIN

Cistercian abbeys all over Europe were built on much the same plan.

EXT. RUINS OF ABBEY. DAY.

Lockwood and Timms smoking somewhere. Hector is asleep under the Sporting Life.

EXT. RUINS OF ABBEY. CLOISTERS. DAY.

Irwin and Dakin observed by Posner and Scripps.

IRWIN

This was where they socialised.

DAKIN

Yes?

IRWIN

Sat in the sun and read. This – (*He indicates an alcove.*) – was where they kept the library.

                    DAKIN
You know it all, don't you?

                    IRWIN
                    (*apologetically*)
It interests me.

                    DAKIN
No, that's good.

It's as if he's the master and Irwin the pupil.

EXT. ABBEY CHANCEL. DAY.

*Crowther break-dancing on the altar. Hector and Mrs Lintott settle down
for their lunch, with a bottle of wine.*

EXT. ELSEWHERE IN THE ABBEY. DAY.

                    TIMMS
All-male community, was it, sir?

                    IRWIN
Of course. They were monks.

                    TIMMS
Bit of that, you think?

                    IRWIN
What?

                    TIMMS
Same-sex stuff?

                    AKHTAR
You've blushed, sir.

                    IRWIN
Have I fuck blushed.

                    CROWTHER
Sir. This is consecrated ground.

                    AKHTAR
Not to me, sir. To me, it's a pagan temple. Only you did blush
a bit, sir.

                    54

LOCKWOOD

Is that why Henry VIII put the boot in, sir? Because of them bunking up?

IRWIN

He said.

LOCKWOOD

Not much else for them to do, was there, sir? I mean in their time off.

POSNER

Pray.

LOCKWOOD

Posner would make a good monk, except he's Jewish.

CROWTHER

Do Jews have monks?

POSNER

Yes, I'm one now.

Hector and Mrs Lintott clink glasses as Irwin and the class arrive.

AKHTAR

That looks good, sir.

HECTOR

It is. It is.

EXT. ABBEY. HIGH ALTAR. DAY.

Akhtar arranges them into a group for a photograph.

HECTOR
(*going towards the high altar*)

Pass the parcel. That's sometimes all you can do. Take it, feel it and pass it on.

Shouts of 'Come on, sir!'

Not for me. Not for you. But for someone, somewhere, one day.

He rejoins the group for the picture.

Pass it on, boys. That's the game I want you to learn. Pass it on.

Akhtar presses the time-delay button and joins the group. A very happy picture.

EXT. SCHOOL. DAY.

The minibus arrives back at the school. They all get out.

INT. CORRIDOR OUTSIDE HEADMASTER'S STUDY. DAY.

Hector and Mrs Lintott trundling rather wearily, possibly with some of the Boys, past the door of the Headmaster's study.

Door opens.

HEADMASTER

Hector. A word.

Hector pulls a face at Mrs Lintott and, if Dakin is there, we maybe see Fiona hovering in the doorway of the office.

INT. HEADMASTER'S STUDY. DAY.

Hector sitting impassively.

HEADMASTER

This is not the first time, apparently, but on this occasion she managed to make a note of the number. For the moment I propose to say nothing about this but fortunately it is not long before you are due to retire. In the circumstances I propose we bring that forward. I think we should be looking at the end of term. Have you nothing to say?

HECTOR

'Then 'twas the Roman; now 'tis I.'

HEADMASTER

This is no time for poetry. I am assuming your wife doesn't know.

HECTOR

I have no idea. What women know or don't know has always
been a mystery to me.

HEADMASTER

And are you going to tell her?

HECTOR

I don't know. I'm not sure she'd be interested.

HEADMASTER

Well, there's another thing. Strange how even the most tragic
turn of events generally resolve themselves into questions about
the timetable. Irwin has been badgering me for more lessons.
In the circumstances a concession might be in order. In the
future, I think you and he might share.

HECTOR

Share?

HEADMASTER

Share. In the meantime you must consider your position. I do
not want to sack you. People talk and it's so untidy. It would be
easier for all concerned if you retired early.

Hector is going.

HECTOR

Nothing happened.

HEADMASTER

A hand on a boy's genitals at fifty miles an hour and you call it
nothing.

HECTOR

The transmission of knowledge is in itself an erotic act. In the
Renaissance . . .

HEADMASTER

Fuck the Renaissance. And fuck literature and Plato and
Michelangelo and Oscar Wilde and all the other shrunken
violets you people line up. This is a school and it isn't normal.

INT. SCHOOL CORRIDOR. DAY.

Hector wanders through the school.

INT. HECTOR'S CLASSROOM. DAY.

Posner waiting in a classroom. Hector pushes the door open.

> HECTOR
>
> Still here?

> POSNER
>
> It is Wednesday, sir.

> HECTOR
>
> Yes, but I thought with the trip to Fountains for the day . . .

> POSNER
>
> It's only half past four.

> HECTOR
>
> In which case, where is Dakin?

> POSNER
>
> With Mr Irwin, sir.

> HECTOR
>
> Of course he is.

> POSNER
>
> He's showing him some old exam questions.

> HECTOR
>
> With the appropriate gobbets, no doubt. No matter. We must carry on the fight without him. What have we learned this week?

> POSNER
>
> 'Drummer Hodge', sir. Hardy.

> HECTOR
>
> Oh. Nice.

Posner says the poem off by heart. At first, Hector's heart doesn't seem to be in listening to it, but Posner draws him in.

'They throw in Drummer Hodge, to rest
Uncoffined – just as found:
His landmark is the kopje crest
That breaks the veldt around;
And foreign constellations west
Each night above his mound.

'Young Hodge the Drummer never knew –
Fresh from his Wessex home –
The meaning of the broad Karoo,
The bush, the dusty loam
And why uprose to nightly view
Strange stars amid the gloam.

'Yet portion of that unknown plain
Will Hodge for ever be;
His homely Northern breast and brain
Grow to some Southern tree,
And strange-eyed constellations reign
His stars eternally.'

HECTOR

Good. Very good. Any thoughts?

Posner sits next to him.

POSNER

I wondered, sir if this 'Portion of that unknown plain will
Hodge for ever be' is like Rupert Brooke, sir. 'There's some
corner of a foreign field.' 'In that dust a richer dust concealed.'

HECTOR

It is. It is. It's the same thought . . . though Hardy's is better,
I think . . . more . . . more, well, down to earth. Quite literally,
yes, down to earth. Anything about his name?

POSNER

Hodge?

It is as if Hector has forgotten everything else except the need to pass it on.

HECTOR

Mmm . . . The important thing is that he has a name. Say
Hardy is writing about the Zulu Wars, or later or the Boer War
possibly, and these were the first campaigns when soldiers . . .
or common soldiers . . . were commemorated, the names of the
dead recorded and inscribed on war memorials. Before this
soldiers – private soldiers anyway – were all unknown soldiers
and, so far from being revered, there was a firm in the nineteenth
century, in Yorkshire of course, which swept up their bones
from the battlefields of Europe in order to grind them into
fertiliser. So, thrown into a common grave though he may be,
he is still Hodge the drummer. Lost boy though he is on the
other side of the world, he still has a name.

POSNER

How old was he?

HECTOR

If he's a drummer he would be a young soldier, not even as old
as you probably.

POSNER

No. Hardy.

HECTOR

Oh, how old was Hardy? When he wrote this, about sixty. My
age, I suppose. Saddish life, though not unappreciated. Uncoffined is a typical Hardy usage. A compound adjective,
formed by putting un- in front of the noun. Or verb, of course.
Un-kissed. Un-rejoicing. Un-confessed. Un-embraced.

It's a turn of phrase that brings with it a sense of not sharing,
of being out of it. Whether because of diffidence or shyness, but
a holding back. Not being in the swim. Can you see that?

POSNER

Yes, sir. I felt that a bit.

A pause.

HECTOR

The best moments in reading are when you come across
something – a thought, a feeling, a way of looking at things –

which you had thought special and particular to you. Now here it is, set down by someone else, a person you have never met, someone even who is long dead. And it is as if a hand has come out and taken yours. Shall we just have the last verse again, and I'll let you go.

With true understanding, Posner recites again the last verse.

POSNER

'Yet portion of that unknown plain
Will Hodge for ever be;
His homely Northern breast and brain
Grow to some Southern tree,
And strange-eyed constellations reign
His stars eternally.'

Dakin comes in.

HECTOR

And now, having thrown in Drummer Hodge as found, here reporting for duty, helmet in hand, is young Lieutenant Dakin.

DAKIN

I'm sorry, sir.

HECTOR

No, no. You were more gainfully employed, I'm sure. Why the helmet?

DAKIN

My turn on the bike. It's Wednesday, sir.

HECTOR

Is it? So it is. But no. Not today. No. Today I go a different way.

'The words of Mercury are harsh after the songs of Apollo. You that way, we this way.'

Hector goes briskly off, leaving Dakin and Posner.

EXT. ROAD. DAY.

Hector, for once alone on his bike, rides by.

EXT. EDGE OF A SUBURBAN WOOD. DAY.

Bikes lean against the wall, both Boys and Girls en route home from their respective schools.

Lockwood is passionately snogging Stephanie, a grammar school girl, while Timms is saddled with her plain friend, Janice.

Janice and Timms watching Lockwood and Stephanie without much interest.

> JANICE
>
> What are you doing about the general paper?

> LOCKWOOD
> (*briefly breaking off*)
>
> What're we not doing about it?

> TIMMS
>
> Yeah. Literature, politics, current affairs. We just bat ideas around the way you do. You can't plan for these things.

> JANICE
>
> Oh, we do, don't we, Stephanie? Mock papers, questionnaires, interviews . . .

> TIMMS
>
> How do you mean, interviews?

> JANICE
>
> 'Self-presentation in the interview set-up'. Miss Harman's got it all worked out.

> TIMMS
>
> Yeah?

> JANICE
>
> General Studies isn't just literature. It's current affairs, sociology, literature as it reflects society. Our school's been sending people to Oxford and Cambridge for years. Stephanie, come on. We'll miss *Timewatch*. It's on the Black Death. What with there being a famine in Ethiopia Miss Harman thinks there might be a comparison question.

Stephanie reluctantly breaks away from Lockwood and she and Janice cycle off.

LOCKWOOD

Why do they always have a fucking friend?

TIMMS

Tony.

LOCKWOOD
(*zipping up his flies*)

What?

TIMMS
(*looking after the girls*)

We're doomed.

INT. HECTOR'S CLASSROOM. DAY.

A somnolent class, the Boys reading, Hector staring into the distance at his desk. Timms looks across to Lockwood and mouths 'Go on' (and one or two of the others seem to know what's coming too).

LOCKWOOD

Sir? Can I say something, sir? We've got this exam coming up, sir, the most important exam of our lives, sir, and we're just sitting here, reading literature.

Hector would normally be fired up by mention of the exam, but isn't.

HECTOR

So?

TIMMS

We've talked it over, sir, and what we think we ought to be doing is like how literature affects society.

LOCKWOOD

Like Jane Austen and the slave trade, sir.

AKHTAR

And interviews, sir. We want to do interviews.

HECTOR
(*who doesn't understand*)

Leaving that aside for the moment, I have something to tell you.

63

AKHTAR

We know all that, sir.

HECTOR

How do you know?

AKHTAR

About sharing classes with Mr Irwin, sir.

HECTOR

No, no. Not that.

LOCKWOOD

Why is that, sir?

HECTOR

It's just a question of the timetable, apparently. No, this is something else.

AKHTAR

Does that mean your lessons will be more like Mr Irwin's, sir?

CROWTHER

More use, sir?

TIMMS

Less farting about?

HECTOR

Hush, boys, hush. Can't you see I'm not in the mood?

DAKIN

What mood is that, sir? The subjunctive? The mood of possibility?

HECTOR

Get on with some work. Read.

LOCKWOOD

That's what we're saying, sir. There's no time for reading now.

TIMMS

Can't you just give us the gist, sir?

AKHTAR

Précis it, sir, like Mr Irwin does.

CROWTHER
Just the outlines, sir, then we can pretend.

HECTOR
Pretend? No, no.

TIMMS
Nobody'll know, sir. That's what exams are for.

HECTOR
Shut up about exams. Shut up the lot of you. You mindless fools. What made me piss my life away in this god-forsaken place? There's nothing of me left. Go away. Class dismissed. Go.

He puts his head down on the desk. There are some giggles and face-pullings before they realise it's serious. Now they're nonplussed and embarrassed. One Boy looks and indicates to the others that Hector is crying. Scripps is nearest to him and ought to touch him but doesn't, and nor does Dakin. Posner is the one who comes and after some hesitation pats Hector rather awkwardly on the back, saying 'Sir.' Then he starts, still very awkwardly, to rub his back.

SCRIPPS
(*to camera*)
I was the nearest. I ought to have been the one to reach out and touch him. But I just watched. Dakin did nothing either. Neither of us did.

He looks at Dakin who looks away.

Later I wrote it all down.

Hector weeping still.

INT. HEADMASTER'S STUDY. DAY.

HEADMASTER
Did he say why he was going?

MRS LINTOTT
More or less.

HEADMASTER
I am surprised. I have said nothing to anyone.

MRS LINTOTT

He would like to stay. To work out his time. That's what I wanted to ask.

HEADMASTER

Shall I tell you what is wrong with Hector as a teacher? It isn't that he doesn't produce results. He does. But they are unpredictable and unquantifiable and in the current educational climate that is no use. He may well be doing his job but there is no method that I know of that enables me to assess the job that he is doing. There is inspiration, certainly, but how do I quantify that? I happened to hear one child singing yesterday morning and on enquiry I find his pupils know all the words of 'When I'm Cleaning Windows'. George Formby. And Gracie Fields. Dorothy, what has Gracie Fields got to do with anything? So the upshot is I am glad he handled his pupils' balls because that at least I can categorise. It is a reason for his going no one can dispute.

Mrs Lintott says nothing.

You didn't know.

MRS LINTOTT

Not that, no.

HEADMASTER

I assumed you knew.

MRS LINTOTT

He handled the boys' balls?

HEADMASTER

I don't want to spell it out. You've been married yourself, you know the form. And while on the motorbike. He, as it were, cradled them. To be fair it was I think more appreciative than investigatory, but it is inexcusable nevertheless. Think of the gulf of years. And the speed! One knows that road well. No, no. It's to everyone's benefit that he should go as soon as possible.

Mrs Lintott leaves the office.

Alan Bennett and Nicholas Hytner

Photographs by Alex Bailey, History Boys Ltd

Nicholas Hytner and Alan Bennett

Alan Bennett, Stephen Campbell Moore, Richard Griffiths and crew

Nicholas Hytner, Alan Bennett and Richard Griffiths

James Corden, Nicholas Hytner and Sacha Dhawan

Russell Tovey and Andrew Knott

Stephen Campbell Moore and Nicholas Hytner

Russell Tovey, Sacha Dhawan and Andrew Knott

Frances de la Tour and Sacha Dhawan

Alan Bennett, Samuel Barnett, Frances de la Tour, Dominic Cooper and Samuel Anderson

Stephen Campbell Moore and Dominic Cooper

Stephen Campbell Moore, Adrian Scarborough and Frances de la Tour

Andrew Dunn, Director of Photography

James Corden and Dominic Cooper

Nicholas Hytner and Alan Bennett

Richard Griffiths and Stephen Campbell Moore

Andrew Dunn

Dominic Cooper, James Corden and Andrew Knott

Dominic Cooper, Andrew Knott and James Corden

Alan Bennett

Jamie Parker, Russell Tovey, Samuel Barnett, Sacha Dhawan,
Samuel Anderson, Dominic Cooper, Andrew Knott and James Corden

Clive Merrison

Richard Griffiths, Samuel Barnett, James Corden and Sacha Dhawan

Richard Griffiths

The history boys

Samuel Barnett, Sacha Dhawan, Penelope Wilton, James Corden
and Russell Tovey

Richard Griffiths

Sacha Dhawan, James Corden, Andrew Knott, Jamie Parker,
Dominic Cooper, Samuel Barnett, Russell Tovey and Samuel Anderson

Dominic Cooper, Samuel Barnett and Samuel Anderson

Clive Merrison and Richard Griffiths

Adrian Scarborough, Jamie Parker and Nicholas Hytner

Nicholas Hytner and Andrew Dunn

Samuel Barnett, Stephen Campbell Moore and Samuel Anderson

Nicholas Hytner, Dominic Cooper, Jamie Parker
and Richard Griffiths

Samuel Barnett, Andrew Knott, Jamie Parker, Dominic Cooper,
Stephen Campbell Moore, Russell Tovey and James Corden
at Fountains Abbey

Samuel Anderson breakdancing at Fountains Abbey

Russell Tovey in the cellarium, Fountains Abbey

The cast at Fountains Abbey

Radcliffe Camera, Oxford

Russell Tovey, Tom Quad, Christ Church, Oxford

Russell Tovey, Dominic Cooper, Samuel Barnett, Jamie Parker
and Sacha Dhawan, Bodleian Library, Oxford

Russell Tovey, Sacha Dhawan, Samuel Barnett, Jamie Parker
and Dominic Cooper, Bodleian Library, Oxford

Mrs Lintott walking alone in the corridor. Small boys stream past her.

MRS LINTOTT
(*to camera*)

I have not hitherto been allotted an inner voice, my role a patient and not unamused sufferance of the predilections and preoccupations of men. They kick their particular stone along the street and I watch. I am, it is true, confided in by all parties, my gender some sort of safeguard against the onward transmission of information . . . though that I should be assumed to be so discreet is in itself condescending. I'm what men would call a safe pair of hands.

She bumps into Irwin.

Our headmaster is a twat. An impermissible word nowadays but the only one suited to my purpose. A twat. And to go further down the same proscribed path, a condescending cunt. Do you think Hector is a good teacher?

IRWIN
Yes, I suppose . . . but what do I know?

MRS LINTOTT
When I taught in London in the seventies there was a myth that not very bright children could always become artists. Droves of the half-educated left school with the notion that art was a viable option. It's by the same well-meaning token that every third person in prison is a potential Van Gogh. There's a bit of that to Hector or else what's all his learning by heart for, except as an insurance against ultimate failure? Not that it matters now, one way or another.

They have reached Hector's classroom.

IRWIN
Why? What's happened?

Her reputation for discretion in jeopardy, the cat nearly out of the bag, Mrs Lintott hastily hits reverse.

Nothing. Nothing. Isn't this his lesson?

IRWIN

It is. But we're sharing, hadn't you heard?

MRS LINTOTT

Sharing? Whose cockeyed idea was that? Don't tell me. Twat, twat, twat.

TIMMS
(*in doorway*)

Yes, miss.

Mrs Lintott goes.

INT. HECTOR'S CLASSROOM. DAY.

Hector, Irwin, the Boys

IRWIN

Would you like to start?

HECTOR

I don't mind.

IRWIN

How do you normally start? It is your lesson. General Studies.

HECTOR

The boys decide. Ask them.

IRWIN

Anybody? The floor is open.

The Boys don't respond.

HECTOR

Come along, boys. Don't sulk.

DAKIN

We don't know who we are, sir. Your class or Mr Irwin's.

IRWIN

Does it matter?

TIMMS

Oh yes, sir. It depends if you want us thoughtful. Or smart.

HECTOR

He wants you civil, you rancid little turd.

Hits him.

TIMMS

Look, sir. You're a witness. Hitting us, sir. He could be sacked.

IRWIN

I thought we might talk about the Holocaust.

HECTOR

Good gracious. But how can you teach the Holocaust?

IRWIN

Well, that would do as a question. Can you . . . should you . . . teach the Holocaust? Anybody?

AKHTAR

It has origins. It has consequences. It's a subject like any other.

SCRIPPS

Not like any other, surely. Not like any other at all.

AKHTAR

No, but it's a topic.

HECTOR

They go on school trips nowadays, don't they? Auschwitz. Dachau. What has always concerned me is where do they eat their sandwiches? Drink their Coke?

CROWTHER

The visitors' centre. It's like anywhere else.

HECTOR

Do they take pictures of each other there? Are they smiling? Do they hold hands? Nothing is appropriate.

LOCKWOOD

What if you were to write that this was so far beyond one's experience silence is the only proper response?

DAKIN

That would be Mr Hector's answer to lots of questions, though, wouldn't it, sir?

HECTOR

Yes. Yes, Dakin, it would.

DAKIN

Whereof one cannot speak thereof one must be silent.

Hector groans and puts his head in his hands.

That's right, isn't it, sir? Wittgenstein.

IRWIN

Yes. That's good.

HECTOR

No, it's not good. It's . . . flip. It's . . . glib. It's journalism.

DAKIN

But it's you that taught us it.

HECTOR

I didn't teach you and Wittgenstein didn't screw it out of his very guts in order for you to turn it into a dinky formula. Why can you not simply condemn the camps outright as an unprecedented horror?

There is slight embarrassment.

LOCKWOOD

No point, sir. Everybody will do that . . . the camps an event unlike any other, the evil unprecedented, etc., etc.

HECTOR

No. Can't you see that even to say *etcetera* is monstrous? *Etcetera* is what the Nazis would have said, the dead reduced to a mere verbal abbreviation.

LOCKWOOD

All right, not *etcetera*. But given that the death camps are generally thought of as unique, wouldn't another approach be to show what precedents there were and put them . . . well . . . in proportion?

SCRIPPS

Proportion!

DAKIN

Not proportion then, but putting them in context.

POSNER

But to put something in context is a step towards saying it can
be understood and that it can be explained. And if it can be
explained then it can be explained away.

RUDGE

'*Tout comprendre c'est tout pardonner.*'

Hector groans.

IRWIN

That's good, Posner.

POSNER

It isn't 'good'. I mean it, sir.

DAKIN

But when we talk about putting them in context it's only
the same as the Dissolution of the Monasteries. After all,
monasteries had been dissolved before Henry VIII, dozens
of them.

POSNER

Yes, but the difference is, I didn't lose any relatives in the
Dissolution of the Monasteries.

IRWIN

Good point.

SCRIPPS

You keep saying, 'Good point.' Not 'good point', sir. True. To
you the Holocaust is just another topic on which we may get a
question.

IRWIN

No. But this is history. Distance yourselves. Our perspective on
the past alters. Looking back, immediately in front of us is dead
ground. We don't see it and because we don't see it this means

that there is no period so remote as the recent past and one of the historian's jobs is to anticipate what our perspective of that period will be . . . even on the Holocaust.

INT. CORRIDOR OUTSIDE HEADMASTER'S STUDY. DAY.

Irwin finds himself overtaken by Dakin and Scripps.

DAKIN

Won the argument there, sir.

IRWIN

What?

DAKIN

The Holocaust. Oh yes. You showed him.

Irwin goes.

SCRIPPS

You flirt.

DAKIN

I don't understand it. I have never wanted to please anybody the way I do him, girls not excepted.

Dakin spots Hector walking disconsolately down the corridor.

He's going, you know.

SCRIPPS

The big man?

DAKIN

Don't let on. Fiona says.

At some point in this scene we see the Posner parents waiting to see the Headmaster, observed without comment by Dakin and Scripps. Then the Headmaster says, 'Mr and Mrs Posner? Come in.'

SCRIPPS

Sacked? Who complained?

Dakin shrugs.

That's why the lifts have stopped.

DAKIN

Poor sod. Though in some ways I'm not sorry.

SCRIPPS

No. No more genital massage as one speeds along leafy suburban roads. No more the bike's melancholy long withdrawing roar as he dropped you at the corner, your honour still intact.

Fiona hurries by, carrying files. A look between her and Dakin.

DAKIN

Lecher though one is, or aspires to be, it occurs to me that the lot of woman cannot be easy, who must suffer such inexpert male fumblings virtually on a daily basis. Are we scarred for life, do you think?

SCRIPPS

We must hope so.

Scripps has stopped by the French Department noticeboard. Proust's photograph in a prominent position.

Perhaps it will turn me into Proust.

INT. HEADMASTER'S STUDY. DAY.

The Headmaster and Irwin.

HEADMASTER

Charming couple, the Posners. Jewish of course.

IRWIN

The boy is clever.

HEADMASTER

Jewish boys often are, though nowadays it's the Asian boys who're out in front, intelligence to some degree the fruit of discrimination. It was apropos the Holocaust.

IRWIN

We did discuss how the Holocaust should be tackled if they got a question on it.

HEADMASTER

And you seem to have said that it should be kept in proportion.

IRWIN

Well, the boys were asking.

HEADMASTER

I'm not concerned with what the boys were asking. What concerns me is what you were telling them.

IRWIN

I was telling them that there were ways of discussing it that went beyond mere lamentation. The risk the historian . . .

HEADMASTER

Mr Irwin. Fuck the historian. These are two angry Jewish parents. I have told them you are young and inexperienced. You will write them a letter of apology on much the same lines. They also complain that Hector has had the boy singing hymns.

IRWIN

Posner likes singing.

HEADMASTER

Hymns?

IRWIN

Anything.

HEADMASTER

Not . . . Gracie Fields?

IRWIN

Possibly.

INT. IRWIN'S CLASSROOM. DAY.

Irwin and Posner.

IRWIN

Do you tell them everything that goes on at school?

POSNER

He's old, my father. He's interested. I just said the Holocaust was a historical fact like other historical facts. It was my uncle who hit me.

Pause.

IRWIN

No more singing, too, I gather?

POSNER

Not hymns. They're fine with Barbra Streisand.

INT. SCHOOL LIBRARY. DAY.

Montage to music: books disappearing from shelves.

INT. VARIOUS SHEFFIELD HOUSES. NIGHT.

At desks, at kitchen tables, the Boys write essays. Close-up on their work as they write.

INT. IRWIN'S CLASSROOM. DAY.

Irwin returns their essays to them.

INT. HISTORY CORRIDOR, LOCKER AREA. DAY.

Dakin, Posner and Scripps are reading what Irwin has written about their latest essays.

DAKIN

Shit. He never gives an inch, does he? 'Lucid and up to a point compelling but if you reach a conclusion it escaped me.'

SCRIPPS

Have you looked at your handwriting recently?

DAKIN

Why?

SCRIPPS

You're beginning to write like him.

DAKIN

I'm not trying to, honestly.

75

You're writing like him, too.

POSNER

No I'm not. Dakin writes like him. I write like Dakin.

DAKIN

It's done wonders for the sex life. Apparently I talk about him
so much Fiona gets really pissed off. Doing it is about the only
time I shut up.

SCRIPPS

Would you do it with him?

DAKIN

I wondered about that. I might. Bring a little sunshine into his
life. It's only a wank, after all.

SCRIPPS

What makes you think he'd do it with you?

Dakin smiles. He is changing his shirt, or otherwise preening himself.

You complacent fuck.

DAKIN

Does the Archbishop of Canterbury know you talk like this?

I like him. I just wish I thought he liked me.

Dakin goes.

POSNER

Irwin does like him. He seldom looks at anyone else.

SCRIPPS

How do you know?

POSNER

Because nor do I. Our eyes meet, looking at Dakin.

SCRIPPS

Oh Poz, with your spaniel heart, it will pass.

POSNER

Yes, it's only a phase. Who says I want it to pass? But the pain.
The pain.

Hector would say it's the only education worth having.

POSNER

I just wish there were marks for it.

INT. FIONA'S BEDROOM. NIGHT.

Fiona lying on a bed, virtually naked.

Dakin stands by the bed without his jacket but otherwise fully clothed. Bad atmosphere. Silence.

FIONA

Do you love him?

DAKIN

Don't be stupid.

FIONA

Well, I don't know, do I?

DAKIN

What do you think this is?

FIONA

Not much, so far.

He starts to get undressed.

Cut to:

Them in bed. She is lying down, him sitting up, hands clasped behind his head. No sex so far, plainly.

DAKIN

I don't fancy him. I just want his approbation, you know.
I want him to rate me.

FIONA

Rape you?

DAKIN

Rate. *Rate.*

Pause.

Fiona?

FIONA

I'm asleep.

Cut to:

Later, when Dakin is asleep.

FIONA
(*sits up and speaks to camera*)
I've an awful feeling this is what life is going to be like, a man
talking about things I don't know or am not interested in,
stopping for a bit while he fucks me then going back to talking
again.

Looks down at Dakin.

Why don't you sleep with him? Have done with it.

Dakin's eyes are open.

INT. MRS LINTOTT'S OR IRWIN'S CLASSROOM. DAY.

*Irwin, Hector and Mrs Lintott, conducting mock interviews. Each boy in
turn sits in the hot seat. The rest look on.*

IRWIN

You're sitting the papers here so there's no need for nerves on
that score. It will be the interviews that decide it. Anything
provocative in your papers and they may question you on that.
Otherwise they are likely to be the usual, 'What are your
hobbies?' type questions.

Crowther is in the hot seat. Mrs Lintott looks at his file.

MRS LINTOTT

Now, Mr Crowther. One of your interests is the theatre. Tell us
about that.

CROWTHER

I'm keen on acting. I've done various parts, favourite being . . .

78

Can I stop you? Don't mention the theatre.

CROWTHER

It's what I'm interested in.

IRWIN

Then soft-pedal it, the acting side of it anyway. Dons . . . most dons . . . think the theatre is a waste of time.

POSNER

Music is all right though, isn't it, sir? They don't frown on that?

HECTOR

No. You should just say what you enjoy.

POSNER

Mozart.

IRWIN

No, no. Everyone likes Mozart. Somebody more off the beaten track. Tippett, say, or Bruckner.

POSNER

But I don't know them.

HECTOR

I have a silly suggestion to make. Why can they not all just tell the truth?

All the Boys react in horror.

MRS LINTOTT

I hesitate to mention this, lest it occasion a sophisticated groan, but it may not have crossed your minds that one of the dons who interviews you may be a woman. I'm reluctant at this stage in the game to expose you to new ideas, but having taught you all history on a strictly non-gender-orientated basis, I just wonder whether it occurs to any of you how dispiriting it is for me to teach five centuries of masculine ineptitude? Am I embarrassing you?

TIMMS

A bit, miss. I mean it's not our fault. It's just the way it is. 'The world is everything that is the case,' miss. Wittgenstein, miss.

MRS LINTOTT

I know it's Wittgenstein, thank you. Why do you think there are no women historians on TV?

TIMMS

No tits?

HECTOR

Hit that boy. Hit him.

TIMMS

Sir! You can't, sir.

HECTOR

I'm not hitting you. He is. And besides, you're not supposed to say tits. Hit him again!

MRS LINTOTT

I'll tell you why. It's because history's not such a frolic for women as it is for men. Why should it be? They never get round the conference table. In 1919, for instance, they just arranged the flowers and then gracefully retired. History is a commentary on the various and continuing incapabilities of men. What is history? History is women following behind with the bucket.

An awkward pause.

IRWIN

Rudge?

Rudge is interviewed.

MRS LINTOTT

Now. How do you define history, Mr Rudge?

RUDGE

Can I speak freely, miss? Without being hit.

MRS LINTOTT

I will protect you.

RUDGE

How do I define history? It's just one fucking thing after another.

Hector makes a moves to hit him but is forestalled.

> MRS LINTOTT
> I see. And why do you want to come to Christ Church?

> RUDGE
> It's the one I thought I might get into.

> IRWIN
> No other reason?

Rudge shakes his head.

> MRS LINTOTT
> Do you like the architecture, for instance?

> RUDGE
> They'll ask me about sport, won't they?

> MRS LINTOTT
> If you're as uncommunicative as this they may be forced to.

> HECTOR
> The point is, Rudge, that even if they want to take you on the basis of your prowess on the field you have to help them to pretend at least that there are other considerations.

> RUDGE
> Look, I'm shit at all this. Sorry.

> If they like me and they want to take me they'll take me because I'm dull and ordinary. I'm no good in interviews but I've got enough chat to take me round the golf course and maybe there'll be someone on the board who wants to go round the golf course. I may not know much about Jean-Paul Sartre but I've got a handicap of four.

> MRS LINTOTT
> Where have you heard about Sartre?

> RUDGE
> He was a good golfer.

> HECTOR
> Really? I never knew that. Interesting.

INT. HISTORY CORRIDOR. DAY – LATER.

The Boys coming away from the mock-interviews.

LOCKWOOD

How did you know Sartre was a golfer?

RUDGE

I don't know that he was. How could I? I don't even know who
the fuck he is. Well, they keep telling us you have to lie.

CROWTHER

I've a feeling Kafka was good at table tennis.

AKHTAR

Yes?

CROWTHER

I'll be glad when we can be shot of all this shit.

EXT. SCHOOL CAR PARK. DAY.

*Dakin catches up with Irwin, who is heading for his car. Boys and teachers
are going home at the end of the day. Dakin gives Irwin an essay.*

DAKIN

Sir, I never gave you my essay.

Irwin takes it. Dakin walks with him.

What degree did you get, sir? You've never said.

IRWIN

A second.

DAKIN

Boring. Didn't the old magic work?

IRWIN

I hadn't perfected the technique.

Dakin offers him a cigarette.

No!

DAKIN

Well, it's after four. I'm going to.

He lights up, smokes.

What college were you at?

IRWIN

Corpus.

DAKIN

That's not one anybody is going in for.

IRWIN

No.

DAKIN

You happy?

IRWIN

There? Yes. Yes, I was quite.

This is quite a pausy conversation with Dakin more master than pupil, and Irwin occasionally having a drag on a cigarette.

DAKIN

Do you think we'll be happy . . . say we get in?

IRWIN

You'll be happy, anyway.

DAKIN

I'm not sure I like that. Why?

Irwin shrugs.

Uncomplicated, is that what you mean? Outgoing? Straight?

IRWIN

None of them bad things to be.

DAKIN

Depends. Nice to be a bit more complicated.

IRWIN

Or to be thought so.

The Headmaster appears, walking towards his car. Dakin pulls Irwin out of sight, round a corner.

DAKIN

You're not very bright.

IRWIN

Am I not?

DAKIN

No, sir.

IRWIN

How's Posner?

DAKIN

Why?

IRWIN

He likes you, doesn't he?

DAKIN

It's his age. He's growing up.

IRWIN

Hard for him.

DAKIN

Boring for me. You're not suggesting I do something about it? It happens. I wouldn't anyway. Too young.

Irwin says nothing.

You still look quite young.

IRWIN

That's because I am, I suppose.

There is an interminable pause.

DAKIN

How do you think history happens?

IRWIN

What?

DAKIN

How does stuff happen, do you think? People decide to do stuff. Make moves. Alter things.

84

IRWIN

I'm not sure what you're talking about.

DAKIN

No?

He smiles.

Think about it.

IRWIN

Some do . . . make moves, I suppose.

Others react to events. In 1939 Hitler made a move on Poland.

Poland / defended itself.

DAKIN
(*overlapping*)

– gave in.

IRWIN

Is that what you mean?

DAKIN
(*unperturbed*)

No. Not Poland anyway. Was Poland taken by surprise?

Dakin should have Irwin practically cornered at this point so that he has to duck out. He heads back to his car.

IRWIN

To some extent. Though they knew something was up. What was your essay about?

DAKIN

Turning points.

IRWIN

Oh yes. Moments when history rattles over the points. Shall I tell you what you've written? Dunkirk?

DAKIN

Yes.

IRWIN

Hitler turning on Russia?

                         DAKIN
Yes.

                         IRWIN
Alamein?

                         DAKIN
Yeah, all those.

                         IRWIN
More? Oh, that's good.

                         DAKIN
When Chamberlain resigned as Prime Minister in 1940
Churchill wasn't the first thought; Halifax more generally
acceptable. But on the afternoon when the decision was taken
Halifax chose to go to the dentist. If Halifax had had better
teeth we might have lost the war.

                         IRWIN
That's terrific.

                         DAKIN
Yeah. It's subjunctive history.

                         IRWIN
Come again.

                         DAKIN
The subjunctive is the mood you use when something might or
might not have happened, when it's imagined.

Hector is crazy about the subjunctive. Why are you smiling?

                         IRWIN
Nothing. Good luck.

Irwin gets into his car, drives off. Dakin leaves school, on top of the world.

INT. SCHOOL HALL. DAY.

*Fiona brings in a sealed envelope. Irwin or Mrs Lintott opens it, distributes
the papers.*

                          86

Rudge looks through the paper, turning it over to check there are questions on the other side. There are not.

> RUDGE

Shit.

Some of the others have already begun to write.

INT. SCHOOL HALL. DAY. LATER.

Mrs Lintott collecting papers, the exam over.

> MRS LINTOTT
> (*as they leave*)

Yes?

> TIMMS

A bit hit-and-miss . . . miss.

> POSNER
> (*ironically*)

I was so nice about Hitler. 'A much misunderstood man.'

> AKHTAR
> (*to Mrs Lintott*)

Queen Elizabeth, miss, less remarkable for her abilities than the fact that, unlike so many of her sisters, she got a chance to exercise them.

> MRS LINTOTT

That's the stuff.

Mrs Lintott hands the papers to Fiona, who puts them in a large envelope, ready to be posted off. Scripps crosses himself.

EXT. SCHOOL. DAY.

A few days later, two minibuses parked outside the school, one marked OXFORD, *one* CAMBRIDGE. *The Boys are climbing in. Hector, Irwin, Mrs Lintott and the Headmaster and several other teachers and boys are there to wave them off. Lockwood, Timms and Crowther are going to Cambridge, the rest to Oxford.*

LOCKWOOD

I hope they don't mind about trainers. They're all I've got.

TIMMS

It's not an examination in footwear.

POSNER

Somebody told me when you go to the bogs it's about four miles.

TIMMS

Listen. Do you want to go to Oxford or do you want
somewhere with a shit degree but with toilets en suite?

RUDGE

What I say is, if they don't like me, then fuck 'em.

TIMMS

Oh Peter, I wish I had your philosophy.

SCRIPPS

And what will you do? Flutter the eyelashes as usual?

DAKIN

No. I think in the circumstances it's the half-smile. A hint of
sadness.

*Scripps reckons to throw up. As the minibus pulls out, Posner starts to sing
'Wish Me Luck As You Wave Me Goodbye', the old Gracie Fields number.
The other Boys join in. The Headmaster glares at Hector.*

INT. WAITING ROOM/FIONA'S OFFICE. DAY.

Irwin and Mrs Lintott are waiting. Fiona isn't there.

IRWIN

What's he want us for?

MRS LINTOTT

No idea.

IRWIN

Pep talk?

MRS LINTOTT

Bit late for that, it's probably about Hector.

IRWIN

I sort of know.

MRS LINTOTT

I imagine everyone sort of knows.

IRWIN

Does his wife?

MRS LINTOTT

He doesn't think so, apparently, but I imagine she's another one who's sort of known all along. A husband on a low light, that's what they want these supposedly unsuspecting wives, the husband's lukewarm attentions just what they married them for. He's a fool. He was also unlucky. The lollipop lady is only on duty a couple of hours. Five minutes later she'd have gone off. And what if there had been no children coming or if the lights had been green? This smallest of incidents, the junction of a dizzying range of alternatives any one of which could have had a different outcome. If I was a bold teacher . . . if I was you, even . . . I could spend a lesson dissecting what the Headmaster insists on calling 'this unfortunate incident' and it would teach the boys more about history and the utter randomness of things than . . . well, than I've ever managed to do so far.

The Headmaster comes in with Hector.

HEADMASTER

Dorothy, a word?

They go.

HECTOR

Trouble at t'mill. That's the news he's aching to impart. My . . . marching orders.

IRWIN

I sort of knew.

HECTOR

Ah.

IRWIN

Dakin told me.

89

Did he tell you why?

Irwin nods.

I've got this idea of buying a van, filling it with books and taking it round country markets . . . Shropshire, Herefordshire. 'The open road, the dusty highway. Travel, change, interest, excitement. Poop, poop.'

Pause.

I didn't want to turn out boys who in later life had a deep love of literature, or who would talk in middle age of the lure of language and their love of words. Words said in that reverential way that is somehow Welsh. That's what the tosh is for. *Brief Encounter*, Gracie Fields, Ivor Novello – it's an antidote. Sheer calculated silliness.

IRWIN

Has a boy ever made you unhappy?

The waiting room should be lined with school photographs, teams etc.

HECTOR

They used to do. See it as an inoculation, rather. Briefly painful but providing immunity for however long it takes. With the occasional booster . . . another face, a reminder of the pain . . . it can last you half a lifetime.

IRWIN

Love.

HECTOR

Who could love me? I talk too much.

IRWIN

Do they know?

HECTOR

They know everything. Don't touch him. He'll think you're a fool.

That's what they think about me.

Mrs Lintott appears.

I gather you knew, too.

Mrs Lintott smiles.

And the boys knew.

MRS LINTOTT
Well, of course the boys knew. They had it at first hand.

HECTOR
I didn't actually do anything. It was a laying on of hands, I
don't deny that, but more in benediction than gratification or
anything else.

MRS LINTOTT
Hector, darling, love you as I do, that is the most colossal balls.

HECTOR
Is it?

MRS LINTOTT
A grope is a grope. It is not the Annunciation. You . . . twerp.
Anyway, what Felix wanted to tell me is that when I finish next
year he's hoping he can persuade you to step into my shoes.

The Headmaster appears.

HEADMASTER
Irwin.

MRS LINTOTT
For your information, they're a size-seven court shoe, broad
fitting.

She kisses Hector.

EXT. OXFORD. DAY.

*Dakin, Scripps, Posner, Akhtar at the Radcliffe Camera exploring Oxford,
walking down Broad Street etc.*

Scripps coming out of a college chapel, noted by two dons.

Rudge in Tom Quad.

EXT. CAMBRIDGE. DAY.

Lockwood, Timms, Crowther walking on The Backs, exploring Cambridge, on King's Parade etc.

A row of boys and girls waiting in the court of one of the colleges, Lockwood's trainers singling him out.

INT. CAMBRIDGE DON'S ROOM. DAY.

Four dons in a book-lined room. One of them goes to the door, calls 'Mr Lockwood'. Lockwood comes in.

INT. OXFORD, CORPUS PORTERS' LODGE. DAY.

Dakin in a college lodge. A Porter looking down a list, shaking his head.

> PORTER
>
> No. No Irwin here.

EXT. OXFORD, CORPUS PORTERS' LODGE. DAY.

Dakin comes out, Scripps is waiting.

> DAKIN
>
> This is Corpus, isn't it?

> SCRIPPS
> *(who is taking photographs)*
>
> Yes.

Dakin looks thoughtful.

EXT. OXFORD COLLEGE. DAY.

Posner and Akhtar, say, at Magdalen New Buildings.

> POSNER
>
> They liked my Hitler answer. Praised what they called my sense of detachment. They said it was the foundation of writing history. My parents would love it, it's like a stately home.

So would mine. They'll never be away. They're already coming
down with fourteen relatives and I haven't even got in.

INT. OXFORD DON'S ROOM. DAY.

*Rudge facing an unencouraging board of Dons and a Sleeping
Clergyman.*

DON

This is Mr Rudge who, if he comes up, is hoping to read
History.

The Sleeping Clergyman mutters to his Neighbour.

NEIGHBOUR

Rudge.

The Sleeping Clergyman looks at Rudge with vague interest.

INTS. VARIOUS SHEFFIELD HOUSES. DAY.

*Envelopes on doormats, say. Scripps, Timms, Crowther opening envelopes,
maybe with their parents in attendance.*

A tiny Asian child bearing an envelope away.

A stick pokes another envelope within reach of the aged Mr Posner.

*Lockwood, astride his bike, opening a mailbox in the entrance to some
council flats.*

INT. HEADMASTER'S STUDY. DAY.

All Boys, except Rudge, celebrating with the teachers.

HEADMASTER

Splendid news! Posner a scholarship, Dakin an exhibition and
places for everyone else. It's more than one could ever have
hoped for. Irwin, you are to be congratulated, a remarkable
achievement. And you too, Dorothy, of course, who laid the
foundations.

MRS LINTOTT

Not Rudge, Headmaster.

HEADMASTER

Not Rudge? Oh dear.

IRWIN

He has said nothing. The others have all had letters.

HEADMASTER

It was always an outside chance. A pity. It would have been good to have a clean sweep. Still, it's like I said all along, you can't polish a turd.

Rudge comes in, sees the carry-on and goes out again. Mrs Lintott goes after him.

INT. CORRIDOR OUTSIDE HEADMASTER'S STUDY. DAY.

MRS LINTOTT

You haven't heard from Oxford?

Rudge shakes his head.

Perhaps you'll hear tomorrow.

RUDGE

Why should I? They told me when I was there.

MRS LINTOTT

I'm sorry.

RUDGE

What for? I got in.

MRS LINTOTT

How come?

RUDGE

How come they told me or how come they took a thick sod like me? I had family connections.

MRS LINTOTT

Somebody in your family went to Christ Church?

94

RUDGE

In a manner of speaking. My dad. Before he got married he
was a college servant there. This old parson who was just sitting
there for most of the interview suddenly said was I related to
Bill Rudge who'd been a scout on Staircase 7 in the 1950s. So
I said he was my dad, and they said I was just the kind of
candidate they were looking for. Mind you, I did all the other
stuff like Stalin was a sweetie and Wilfred Owen was a wuss.
They said I was plainly someone who thought for himself and
just what the college rugger team needed.

MRS LINTOTT

Are you not pleased?

RUDGE

It's not like winning a match.

She is turning away.

You see, miss, I want to do stuff I want to do. This, I only
wanted it because the others did. And my dad. Now I've got in
I just feel like telling the college to stuff it.

MRS LINTOTT

I think that's Mr Hector.

RUDGE

No, it isn't, miss. It's me.

INT. IRWIN'S CLASSROOM. DAY.

Dakin comes in. Irwin is working.

DAKIN

I went round to your college.

IRWIN

I'm surprised you were interested.

DAKIN

I was kind of lonely. I wanted to see where you'd been. Only
nobody'd heard of you at Corpus.

IRWIN

I said I was at Jesus.

DAKIN

Corpus.

IRWIN

Corpus, Jesus. What does it matter?

Pause.

I never got in. I was at Bristol.

I did go to Oxford, but it was just to do a teaching diploma. Does that make a difference?

DAKIN

To what? To me? (*He shrugs.*) At least you lied. And lying's good, isn't it? We've established that. Lying works. Except you ought to learn to do it properly.

Pause.

Anybody else, I'd say we could have a drink.

Irwin doesn't respond.

Is that a euphemism? Saying a drink when you actually mean something else?

IRWIN

It is, yes.

DAKIN

Actually, forget the euphemism.

I'm just kicking the tyres on this one but, further to the drink, what I was really wondering was whether there were any circumstances in which there was any chance of your sucking me off.

Pause.

Or something similar.

Pause.

Actually, that would please Hector.

What?

DAKIN

'Your sucking me off.' It's a gerund. He likes gerunds. And your being scared shitless, that's another gerund.

IRWIN

I didn't know you were that way inclined.

DAKIN

I'm not, but it's the end of term; I've got in to Oxford; I thought we might push the boat out.

Pause.

Anyway I'll leave it on the table.

He is ready to go but turns back.

I don't understand this.

Reckless; impulsive; immoral . . . how come there's such a difference between the way you teach and the way you live? Why are you so bold in argument and talking, but when it comes to something that's actually happening, I mean now, you're so fucking careful? Is it because you're a teacher and I'm . . . a boy?

IRWIN

Obviously that . . .

DAKIN

Why? Who cares? I don't.

IRWIN

You've already had to cope with one master who touches you up. I don't . . .

DAKIN

Is that what it is? Is it that you don't want to be like Hector?

You won't be. You can't be. How can you be? Hector's a joke.

IRWIN

No, he isn't. He isn't.

DAKIN

That side of him is.

IRWIN

This . . . it's . . . it's such a cliché.

DAKIN

Not to me, it isn't. Go on. Be a devil.

Irwin takes out his diary.

No. Don't take out your sodding diary. God, we've got a long way to go. Do you ever take your glasses off?

IRWIN

Why?

DAKIN

It's a start.

IRWIN

Not with me. Taking off my glasses is the last thing I do.

DAKIN

Yes? I'll look forward to it.

What do you do on a Sunday afternoon? What are you doing this Sunday afternoon?

Dakin opens Irwin's shirt. Maybe puts a hand inside.

IRWIN

Well, I was going to go through the accounts of Roche Abbey. It was a Cistercian house just to the south of Doncaster.

DAKIN

Oh yes? What about Monday? Monday's kind of a dumb night, but it'll do. Only remember –

And here he fastens Irwin's shirt button again as if Irwin's a child.

– we're not in the subjunctive any more either. It's going to happen.

Cut to:

INT. CORRIDOR OUTSIDE THE HEADMASTER'S STUDY. DAY.

Dakin and a horrified Scripps.

DAKIN

I just wanted to say thank you.

SCRIPPS

So? Give him a subscription to the *Spectator* or a box of Black
Magic. Just because you've got a scholarship doesn't mean
you've got to give him unfettered access to your dick.

DAKIN

So how would you say thank you?

SCRIPPS

The same probably. On my knees.

I shall want a full report.

DAKIN

Are you jealous? You are, aren't you?

SCRIPPS

Not of the sex. Just of your being up for it. Me . . . I'm . . .

DAKIN

Write it down.

*They are passing the Headmaster's study and Dakin suddenly knocks at
the door.*

Wish me luck.

SCRIPPS

What for?

Dakin draws his finger across his throat as the Headmaster says 'Come in.'

INT. HEADMASTER'S STUDY. DAY.

HEADMASTER

Now, Dakin, how can I help?

INT. FIONA'S OFFICE. DAY.

Fiona listening, hands half over her eyes.

INT. HEADMASTER'S STUDY. DAY.

> HEADMASTER
> I've never known such impertinence.
>
> Your scholarship seems to have gone to your head.

> DAKIN
> The point I'm making, sir . . .

> HEADMASTER
> I know the point you're making.

> DAKIN
> I'm just curious, sir. What is the difference between Mr Hector feeling us up on a motorbike and your touching up Fiona? Or trying to. A comparable situation historically would be the dismissal of Cardinal Wolsey.

> HEADMASTER
> Don't give me that Cardinal Wolsey shit. Who else knows about this?

INT. FIONA'S OFFICE. DAY.

Dakin is coming out of the study. The Headmaster behind him.

> HEADMASTER
> Fiona . . . Miss Proctor. Mr Hector to my study please.

EXT. SCHOOL. DAY.

Dakin and Scripps coming through one of the school entrances.

> DAKIN
> What else could he do? I had him by the scrotum. Fiona's not pleased, of course. 'It puts me in an awkward position.'

> SCRIPPS
> (*to camera*)
> I remember saying, 'So everybody's happy,' and the exact place

where I said it, and knowing, even at eighteen, that this was an unwise thing to say. Because, sure enough, after that things began to unravel pretty quickly.

EXT. SCHOOL CAR PARK. DAY.

The Boys are leaving.

> LOCKWOOD
> I might try the army.

> TIMMS
> You? You're a shambles.

> LOCKWOOD
> I know, but they put you through college apparently. Fees, everything.

> AKHTAR
> Yeah, provided you kill people afterwards.

> LOCKWOOD
> We won't go to war again. Who is there to fight?

> SCRIPPS
> I don't know about a career. I've got to get fucking out of the way first.

> CROWTHER
> That goes on.

> POSNER
> Or doesn't.

Dakin arrives.

> DAKIN
> Now look, everybody. This is known as Posner's reward.

He hugs Posner.

> POSNER
> Is that it? The longed-for moment?

> DAKIN
> What's wrong with it?

Too fucking brief. I was looking for something more . . .
lingering.

*Dakin does it again. They are parted, Dakin is carrying the motorbike
helmet.*

And what's this, Hector's reward?

DAKIN

I thought I would. It's only polite. Just for old time's sake.

SCRIPPS

Just don't let him go past the lollipop lady.

Hector comes by in his leathers, beaming.

DAKIN
(*helmet on*)

Ready, sir?

HECTOR

Oh, Dakin . . .

DAKIN

Think of it as a gesture, sir.

HECTOR

But I'm not leaving, I shall be back next year . . .

Headmaster arrives.

HEADMASTER

What is this? A boy in a motorcycle helmet? Who is it? Dakin?

No, no, no. Under no circumstances.

Hector, I thought I'd made this plain.

Hector (whose fault it isn't, after all) just shrugs.

Take somebody else . . . take –

Irwin has arrived.

Take Irwin.

HECTOR

Irwin?

Sure, why not?

Dakin gives him the helmet.

DAKIN

Do you want my *Tudor Economic Documents*?

IRWIN

Fuck. Off. Fuck right off.

EXT. ROAD. DAY.

The bike roars by, Hector and Irwin on it.

EXT. SCHOOL. DAY.

SCRIPPS
(*to camera*)

They hadn't gone far. If you'd been listening you might have heard it.

INT. MRS LINTOTT'S CLASSROOM. DAY.

Mrs Lintott looks up from some marking, then goes back to her books.

EXT. SCHOOL. DAY.

Rudge, teeing up a rugger ball, say, looks up, then kicks the ball. Some of the other Boys, unlocking bikes, vaguely register something.

An ambulance siren.

SCRIPPS
(*to camera*)

There are various theories about what happened, why he came off. It's inconceivable he ever touched Irwin who would in any case have been clutching his briefcase. Or it may be Hector was so used to driving with one hand while the other was busy behind him that driving with two made him put on speed.

EXT. ROAD. DAY.

The bike on its side. An ambulance, police cars. A small crowd.

> SCRIPPS
> (*voice-over*)
> These explanations are a touch obvious which, if he taught us anything, Irwin taught us not to be. So I think that, since Irwin had never been on the back of a bike before, going round the corner he leaned out instead of in and so unbalanced Hector. That would be appropriate, too. Trust Irwin to lean the opposite way to everyone else.

INT. SCHOOL HALL. DAY.

Hector's memorial service. A full house of boys, teachers and parents taking their places. The History Boys are in the front row. Irwin hobbles to his place beside them, leg in plaster, on crutches.

> IRWIN
> (*to camera*)
> With no memory of what happened I am of no help. I only know what I have been told, my last memory Dakin asking me for a drink. Something we never did, incidentally.

He has taken his place not far from Dakin.

> DAKIN
> (*to camera*)
> Still. At least I asked him. And barring accidents it would have happened.

> RUDGE
> Listen, you stupid cunt, there is no barring accidents. It's what I said. History is just one fucking thing after another.

> SCRIPPS
> Someone dies at school and you remember it all your life.

INT. SCHOOL HALL. DAY.

Later. The History Boys are on stage, singing 'Bye Bye Blackbird'. Behind them a large screen: images of Hector in youth and middle age are projected onto it.

INT. SCHOOL HALL. DAY.

The Headmaster is now at the lectern.

> HEADMASTER
>
> If I speak of Hector it is of enthusiasm shared, passion conveyed and seeds sown of future harvest. He loved language. He loved words. For each and every one of you, his pupils, he opened a deposit account in the bank of literature and made you all shareholders in that wonderful world of words.

During his speech the camera finds Mrs Lintott, sitting with the History Boys, who are now seated again.

> MRS LINTOTT
> *(to camera)*
> Will they come to my funeral, I wonder? And what will they be?

She turns to Akhtar.

> Akhtar, what are you?

> AKHTAR
> Headmaster, miss. In Keighley, near Bradford.

> MRS LINTOTT
> One of you is a magistrate, I know.

Crowther raises a weary hand. The hall is now empty except for the History Boys, Mrs Lintott and Irwin. The light has changed.

> And Timms, what are you?

> TIMMS
> Chain of dry cleaners, miss. And I take drugs at the weekend.

> MRS LINTOTT
> And are you all happy?

They look at one another, shrug and with some diffidence, and the odd abstention, acknowledge that they are, pretty much.

> TIMMS
> Kids don't help, though, miss.

> MRS LINTOTT
> Dakin, you're happy, I'm sure.

DAKIN

Of course, miss, I'm a tax lawyer. The money's incredible.

MRS LINTOTT

Despite knowing with Wittgenstein that the world is everything that is the case, Lieutenant Anthony Lockwood of the York and Lancaster Regiment is wounded by friendly fire and dies on his way to hospital. He is twenty-eight.

Lockwood puts both hands up.

RUDGE

'Tout comprendre c'est tout pardonner.'

MRS LINTOTT

Ah, Rudge, I'd forgotten you.

RUDGE

As usual, miss.

MRS LINTOTT

You're a builder, carpeting the dales in handy homes.

RUDGE

Rudge Homes are affordable homes for the first-time buyer. I take wives round the Show House. I tell them I was at Oxford and I get fucks galore.

MRS LINTOTT

There is one journalist, though on a better class of paper, a career he is always threatening to abandon in order, as he puts it, 'really to write'.

Scripps puts up his hand. Irwin, now without his crutches, rises.

IRWIN

Hector always said I was a journalist.

MRS LINTOTT

And so you were. School was just an apprenticeship for television. I enjoy your programmes, but they're more journalism than history.

She has moved towards Posner.

Of all Hector's boys there is only one who truly took everything to heart, remembers everything he was ever taught . . . the

songs, the poems, the sayings, the endings – the words of
Hector never forgotten.

> POSNER

Slightly to my surprise I've ended up, like you, a teacher. I'm
a bit of a stock figure . . . I do a wonderful school play, for
instance . . . and though I never touch the boys, it's always a
struggle, but maybe that's why I'm a good teacher. I'm not
happy, but I'm not unhappy about it.

> MRS LINTOTT

So why do you teach?

> POSNER

I . . . share.

Hector is there, but nobody can see him. He talks to Mrs Lintott.

> HECTOR

Finish, good lady, the bright day is done and we are for the dark.

> IRWIN

He was a good man but I do not think there is time for his kind
of teaching any more.

> SCRIPPS

No. Love apart, it is the only education worth having.

They all start slowly to leave the hall, leaving behind the unseeable Hector.

> HECTOR

Pass the parcel. That's sometimes all you can do. Take it, feel it
and pass it on. Not for me, not for you but for someone,
somewhere, one day.

EXT. ABBEY, HIGH ALTAR. DAY.

*They are back at the ruined abbey, on the day of the class outing, in
position for the happy group photograph. Shouts of 'Come on, sir!'*

Pass it on, boys. That's the game I wanted you to learn. Pass it on.

End.

ALAN BENNETT has been one of Britain's leading dramatists since the success of *Beyond the Fringe* in the 1960s. His television series *Talking Heads* has become a modern-day classic, as have many of his works for the stage, including *Forty Years On*, *The Lady in the Van*, *A Question of Attribution*, *The Madness of George III* (together with the Oscar-nominated screenplay *The Madness of King George*), and an adaptation of Kenneth Grahame's *The Wind in the Willows*. At the National Theatre, London, *The History Boys* won numerous awards, including *Evening Standard* and Critics' Circle awards for Best Play, an Olivier Award for Best New Play, and the South Bank Award. On Broadway, *The History Boys* won five New York Drama Desk Awards, including Outstanding New Play; four Outer Critics' Circle Awards; a New York Drama Critics' Award for Best Play; a New York Drama League Award for most distinguished production of a play; and six Tony Awards, including Best Play. His latest collection of prose, *Untold Stories*, won the PEN/Ackerley Prize for autobiography, 2006. Alan Bennett was named the Reader's Digest Author of the Year, 2005.

NICHOLAS HYTNER is Director of the National Theatre in London. Since 1989 he has directed all of Alan Bennett's plays and screenplays: *The Wind in the Willows*, *The Madness of George III* and the film *The Madness of King George*, *The Lady in the Van*, and *The History Boys* on stage and screen. His productions at the National include: *Ghetto*, *The Recruiting Officer*, *Carousel*, *The Cripple of Inishmaan*, *The Winter's Tale*, *Mother Clap's Molly House*, *Henry V*, *His Dark Materials*, *Stuff Happens*, *Henry IV Parts 1 and 2*, *Southwark Fair*, and *The Alchemist*. His films include *The Crucible*.